Facts about
Norway

15 th EDITION

2. printing 1976

CHR. SCHIBSTEDS FORLAG · OSLO

Contents

Notes on History	3
Country and People	5
The Country	5
Climate	6
Population	7
Main Cities	8
Government	9
The Constitution	9
The King	10
Parliament	10
The Cabinet	12
Administration	13
Post War Politics	15
International Relations	16
Justice	17
Defence	19
Finances	20
The Public Sector	20
The Banks	21
Credit Market	22
Insurance	23
Economy	23
General Survey	23
Agriculture	24
Forestry	26
Fisheries	27
Sealing	30
Power Supply	30
Mining and Quarrying	34
Manufacturing Industries	35
Shipping	38
Sea Rescue	42
Foreign Trade	42
Communications	44
Roads	44
Railways	45
Aviation	45
Coastal Transport	46
Postal Service	47
Telecommunications	47
Mass Media	47
The Press	47
Radio and Television	48
Health	49
Social Conditions	51
The National Insurance	51
Social Care	55
Child Welfare	55
Labour Protection	56
Education	57
Primary Schools	57
Secondary Schools	58
Education of Teachers	60
Universities and Equivalent Institutions	60
Science and Research	62
Culture	63
Language	63
Literature	63
Book Publishing	64
Libraries	64
Theatre	64
Music	65
Opera	66
Film	66
Fine Arts	67
Architecture	69
Applied Arts and Design	70
Government Support	71
Religion	72
Sports and Recreation	73
Outdoor Recreation	73
Competitive Sports	73
Tourism in Norway	75
Standard of Living	75
Books on Norway in English	78

Facts about Norway – 15th edition 1975. Second printing 1976.
1st – 15th edition: 327 000 copies printed.
Published by the newspaper Aftenposten, Oslo,
in co-operation with the Royal Ministry of Foreign Affairs.
Editor: Ola Veigaard.
© by Chr. Schibsteds Forlag, Oslo 1976.
Printed in Norway by Naper Boktrykkeri, Kragerø.
ISBN 82–516–0577–6

The statistics contained in the booklet are based on the latest available official figures and data. Where not otherwise specified English weights and measurements are used. All values are stated in Norwegian kroner (kr.). In the currency of some other countries the approx. value of 100 kroner is: £ 9.40, US $ 18, Canadian $ 17.7, D.M. 45.9, Swiss francs 45.9, French francs 84.4, Dutch gulden 48.5, Italian lire 15.220. (All exchange quotations are nominal.)

Notes on History

800–900. Activities of the Vikings increase. The small Norwegian agrarian communities are organized into larger administrative and military regions.

875 (approx.). Small Viking settlements established in the Hebrides, the Isle of Man, the Shetlands and the Orkneys, England, Ireland and Normandy.

900 (approx.). Unification of the Realm. Battle of Hafrsfjord. King Harald Hårfagre (Fairhair) first supreme ruler of all Norway.

1000 (approx.). Greenland and America discovered, the latter by Leiv Eriksson. Christianity introduced to Norway. Norway intermittently under Danish rule.

1030. King Olav Haraldsson killed in battle when trying to re-establish himself as king of Norway. Later on becomes Norway's patron saint. Consolidation of the monarchy under his son, Magnus (the Good), who 1042–47 is also king of Denmark.

1066. King Harald Hårdråde killed in battle of Stamford Bridge in the attempt to become king of England. This was the last Viking raid.

1130–1240. The dual system of succession, combining heredity and election, leads to civil war.

1152. Norway becomes separate bishopric, with archbishop's see at Nidaros (Trondheim).

1163. First coronation of a Norwegian king (Magnus V). Under new law of succession the Church is to decide between pretenders to the throne.

1194. King Sverre Sigurdsson comes into conflict with the Church and is excommunicated by the Pope.

1217–1263. End of civil wars, followed by a period of greatness for Norway (Iceland and Greenland dependencies of the Crown), also culturally – Snorre Sturlasson writes the Norwegian sagas.

1274–1276. King Magnus «Lawmender» codifies the laws of Norway.

1319–1360. Personal union with Sweden.

1349–1350. «Black Death» wipes out half the population. Economy deteriorates. Hanseatic merchants dominate trade.

1380. Union with Denmark which lasts till 1814.

1397. Union of Kalmar. Sweden joins the Danish-Norwegian union. The triple union continues, with intervals, until 1521.

1468–1469. The Orkney and the Shetland Islands mortgaged to the King of Scotland.

1563–1570. Nordic Seven Years' War.

1709–1721. Nordic Great War.

1807–1814. War against England and Sweden. Blockade and famine.

1811. First Norwegian university founded, opened 1813.

1814. Sweden forces Denmark to cede Norway. Norwegians refuse to recognize treaty. National Assembly convenes and adopts Constitution (May 17th), Danish prince elected King of Norway. War with Sweden July-August. King resigns and the first Norwegian Storting agrees to union with Sweden (1814–1905).

1837. Municipal self-government introduced.

1866–1973. First great emigration period with more than 100,000 emigrants, mainly to USA.

1884. Parliamentary government introduced.

1887. Jury system introduced.

1898. Universal male suffrage.

1900–1910. Second great emigration period (200,000 emigrants). Total overseas emigration from Norway: 880,000.

1905. Union with Sweden dissolved and Norway becomes independent. Prince Carl of Denmark elected King and takes the name of Haakon VII.

1913. Women's Parliamentary suffrage.

1914–18. Norway neutral in World War I, but merchant navy suffers great losses.

17th May, Constitution Day, the National Day of Norway, is celebrated with children's processions all over the country.

1925. Svalbard (Spitsbergen) placed under Norwegian sovereignty.

1940. Germany invades Norway April 9th. Fighting in Southern Norway until May 5th and in Northern Norway until June 7th. The King, the Crown Prince and the Government leave the country with the authority of Storting to continue the fight from London.

1940–45. Small Norwegian fighting units transferred from Norway form the nuclei of the Free Norwegian Forces, which are reinforced by recruits escaped from occupied Norway, Norwegians abroad and the merchant navy. Regime of terror, with concentration camps, introduced by Nazis, reprisals following acts of sabotage, and executions of political prisoners and hostages. In 1944, Norwegian refugees in Sweden set up fighting force.

1945. Surrender of German forces May 8th. The Storting ratifies UN Charter November 16th.

1949. Norway joins NATO.

1952. The Nordic Council, consisting of parliamentarians from Denmark, Finland, Iceland, Norway and Sweden, is established.

1957. King Haakon VII dies and is succeeded by Olav V.

1959. Norway joins the European Free Trade Association (EFTA).

1962 and **1967.** Norway applies for membership of the European Community (EC).

1970. Norway starts negotiations with EC.

1972. In an advisory referendum on Common Market membership Norway says NO to joining EC.

1973. Trade agreement with EC ratified by Norway.

Country and People

Area: Norway (in Norwegian: *Norge* – originally *Nordvegr*, meaning «the northern way») is situated between 57° 57' 31" N and 71° 11' 8" N latitude and between 4° 30' 13" E and 31° 10' 4" E longitude, with an area of 323 883 sq. km (125.018 sq. miles). In addition, there are the territories of Svalbard (Spitsbergen) (62,050 sq. km, eq. 23,958 sq. miles) and the island of *Jan Mayen* (373 sq km, eq. 144 sq. miles) in the Artic, and in the Antarctic *Peter I Island* and the *Bouvet Island* (totalling 308 sq. km, eq. 119 sq. miles), as well as a sector of the Antarctic continent, lying between 20° W and 45° E longitude, *Queen Maud Land.*

The Country

Norway constitutes the western part of the Scandinavian peninsula, of which it covers about 40 %. The country is the fifth largest in Europe, while population density is next-lowest in Europe, after Iceland. In the east the country borders on Sweden, Finland and the Soviet Union, and otherwise has the sea as its boundary, with an exceptionally long coast line. Along the coast there are numerous islands (about 50,000, of which only 2,000 are inhabited) and nearly three quarters of the area is unsuitable for habitation or cultivation.

Oslo, the capital lies about 60° N. This latitude runs north of Scotland, through central Canada and southern Alaska. Norway's most northern town, Hammerfest, is also the most northerly in the world, lying on 70° 39' 48" N latitude. The Arctic Circle crosses near the middle of Norway. Northern Norway is well known to tourists as "The land of the Midnight Sun."

Topography

Four fifths of Norway is more than 150 metres above sea level, the average height a.s.l. being 500 metres (compared with 300 metres in the rest of Europe). In spite of this, most of the topography is not alpine. Most of the country consists of treeless high plateaux, with numerous lakes, one of them Lake Hornindalsvatn, the deepest lake in Europe. The land area of which Norway is a part, slopes gradually towards the east and drops steeply into the sea in the west.

The *Dovre* Mountains, the general direction of which is W–E, divide the country naturally in a northern and a southern part, while the latter is divided in a western and an eastern part by the *Langfjellene* Mountains (N–S). The mountain chain *Kjølen* runs N–S along the greater part of the Norwegian-Swedish border.

Glaciers and rivers of the Ice Age cut *valleys* in the mountains, long and sloping towards east and south, short and steep towards the west. They are continued by the *fjords*, which are usually narrow and penetrate far into the country – as far as 183 kilometres.

There are 1700 glaciers in Norway, covering a total area of 1 300 sq. miles.

The highest *waterfalls* are found in western Norway. The rivers of the interior do not run so swiftly, but many of these falls have a greater volume of water.

Flora and Fauna

Norway's flora is richer (about 2,000 species) than might be expected from the country's location. Most of the plants are also found in other countries, with only a few mountain plants being peculiar to Norway.

The predominating trees in Norwegian forests, which cover nearly one quarter of the country, are *spruce* and *pine*, but *birch* and other deciduous trees are found even in mountainous districts. Vegetation is richest in the southeastern districts, the deep forests of the main valleys forming the basis of Norwegian lumber industry. The conifers are seldom found above 800–1,000 m. Wild berries, particularly *blueberries* and *cranberries*, grow in the woodlands. *Cloudberries*, which are little known outside Scandinavia, are gathered in the mountains.

Of animal life, the marine fauna is of considerable importance to the country, large districts being almost entirely dependent on fisheries. Of land animals the *bear* is almost extinct, while *elk* is found mainly in southeastern Norway and Trøndelag. *Reindeer* is the most important domestic animal in Finnmark. There are many species of animals of prey, such as *wolf, fox, lynx, otter*. Game birds are found both in the valleys and in the mountains, the *ptarmigan* (grouse) being the most common. Fresh water fish such as *trout* are found in practically all rivers and lakes throughout the country, while *salmon* is rarely caught elsewhere than in certain typical "salmon rivers".

Multitudes of sea birds nest on the coast of northern Norway. The nesting cliffs on the west and north coast, which are inhabited by thousands of birds, are among the country's tourist attractions.

Many of the birds of Norway are migratory, hatching in Norway, but living in more southern parts of the world for most of the year. Migration is also common with certain species of fish such as mackerel.

Bear and wolf are totally protected, while wolverine is protected only in southern Norway.

National Parks

Norwegians are in the happy position of having access to practically all lake and sea shores, and to vast forest lands and mountain areas. About 96 per cent of the country is open to the general public.

However, the increasing demands of a growing population for sites for housing, roads and development of hydro-electric plants are having detrimental effects on forests, lakes, flora and wildlife.

The conservation of these assets is increasingly becoming a public issue, and several private societies as well as government agencies have been formed for this purpose. Since 1962, eleven areas have been designated National Parks, and there are plans for adding to their number. *Rondane* and *Børgefjell* are among the the most famous. A great many areas, of interest because of their flora and fauna, are or will be protected by law as nature reserves. Three national parks, two nature reserves and fifteen bird sanctuaries have been established in Svalbard.

Climate

There are many different types of climate in Norway. This is so on account of the country's geographical situation between 58° and 71° N, because of the varying topography, and because of strong prevailing westerly winds and the Gulf Stream along the west coast of Norway.

Along the entire length of the west coast from Lindesnes to Lofoten, the climate is exceptionally mild during the winter, with mean temperatures of 1–2 °C. In Lofoten, mean temperature in January is low. In Finnmark, mean temperature in the winter is about ÷ 14° C, on the Røros high plateau it is about ÷ 10° C. Along the coast, mean temperature in the summer is not very high, about 13–14° C in southern Norway, and about 9° C in East Finnmark. The districts around Oslo and the Oslo Fjord have the highest mean temperature, 15–17° C. The highest temperature ever recorded in Norway is 35.6° C, the lowest ÷ 51°C.

Because of the prevailing westerly winds, the western part of Norway receives the greatest amount of precipitation. Some districts in that part of the country get about 3,000 mm annually, whereas a few inland districts get only 300–400 mm annually.

Inland, wind force is generally low.

Some Meteorological Data

	Mean temperatures			Extreme temperatures		Pre-
	Annual	January	July	Max.	Min.	cip.*
Oslo	5.9 (43)	–4.7 (34)	17.3 (63)	35.0 (95)	–26.4 (–16)	42 in
Bergen ...	7.8 (46)	1.5 (35)	15.0 (59)	31.8 (89)	–15.1 (+5)	126 »
Trondheim	4.9 (41)	–3.4 (26)	14.4 (58)	35.0 (95)	–26.1 (–15)	49 »
Tromsø ..	2.9 (37)	–3.5 (26)	12.4 (54)	30.2 (86)	–18.4 (– 1)	59 »

Temperatures in centigrade (Fahrenheit equivalents in brackets)

* Max. precipiation in one year. The coldest areas are the Finnmark and Røros plateaux which on the average have 230—245 days a year with a temperature below freezing point. Highest recorded temperature in Norway is 35.6⁰ C = 96⁰ F, (Nesbyen), lowest ÷ 51.4⁰ C = ÷ 61⁰ F (Karasjok).

In the mountains and along the coast, in the western and northern parts of the country especially, high wind forces may occur. In those districts, wind forces of 4–5 on the Beaufort scale are not unusual during the winter, and every year gales of force 9 or higher in the Beaufort scale occur somewhere or other along the coast.

The Midnight Sun

The midnight sun (whole disc) is visible at the North Cape from 14 May till 29 July (approx.), and is seen for a shorter period throughout northern Norway.

Population

Population: 4,017,231 (1976, estimated), which is equal to 12,4 inhabitants per sq. km (32,13 per sq. mile)–the dependencies not included. Or, to put it in another way – if the area were divided equally, there would be almost 100,000 sq. metres (eq. 25 acres) for each Norwegian.

During the last decade a number of areas around the country have been designated National Parks. This scenery can be seen in one of the parks in southern Norway, Gutulia on Lake Femunden.

7

Vital Statistics

	1901–05	1936–40	1949–50	1951–55	195(
Live births per 1000 population	28,5	15,4	20,6	18,6	17
Marriages per 1000 population	6,1	8,5	9,0	8,0	6
Average age at first marriage Men ...	27,7	29,3	29,3	28,5	27
Women	25,7	26,4	26,4	25,5	24
Divorces per 100 marriages	1,3	4,3	7,7	7,7	9
Deaths per 1000 population	14,6	10,3	9,1	8,5	8
Deaths during first year per 1000 live births..........................	66,3	39,4	31,1	22,6	19
Excess of births over deaths per 1000 population	13,9	5,1	11,5	10,1	9
Emigration to overseas countries per 1000 inhabitants	9,0	0,2	0,6	0,8	0
Increase of population per 1000 inhabitants	6,2	5,9	10,8	9,7	8
Expectation of life Men...........	54,8	64,1	69,3	71,1	71
Women	57,7	67,6	72,7	74,7	75

*) Statistics concerning emigration has not been made since 1965.

Growth of Population

Year	1769	1801	1825	1845	1865	1890	1900	19
Total in 1000........	728	883	1 051	1 329	1 702	2 001	2 240	2 8
In towns, %	8,9		10,9		15,6		28,8	

Approx. 55 % of the population live in rural districts, 45 % in towns and built-up areas.

Man has lived in Norway for at least 10,000 years, but the country did not become really settled until historical times. The majority of the population today belong to the Nordic race – tall, fair, long-skulled people, and most of them have blue eyes. On the west and south coasts the population is of intermixed Alpine and Nordic stock, while here and in the southeastern forest districts, and in the far north there are also a number of people of Baltic origin, whose ancestors immigrated from Finland. In northern Norway the latter group (kvener), about 7,000 in number, has maintained its distinctive characteristics. In the north there is also a minority group of about 20,000 Lapps (samer), whose culture and language differ greatly from Norwegian culture and language. Dark hair, dark eyes and short stature are some of the anthropological characteristics often found in the population of the far north, and are an inheritance from the Lapps, who have been living there since pre-historic days.

According to statistics, 80 % of the Norwegian conscripts have blue eyes or fair hair, and average height has increased about 9 cm since 1900 to 179,0 cm (approx. 5 ft 10 in) in 1973.

Norway has, together with the other Scandinavian countries and the Netherlands, the highest expectation of life in the world.

Main Cities

Oslo, the capital of Norway, has a population of 464,900 and covers a total area of 175 sq. miles. Founded about 1048. Seat of the King,

1–65	1966–70	1971	1972	1973
,5	17,5	16,8	16,3	15,5
,6	7,6	7,6	7,3	7,1
,0	24,8	24,6	24,6	24,6
,9	22,3	22,2	22,2	22,2
,3	10,4	12,6	14,1	16,6
,5	9,8	10,0	10,0	10,1
,1	13,1	12,8	11,8	–
,0	7,7	6,8	6,3	5,4
,3*				
,8	7,0	7,6	7,8	6,3
,0	71,1	–	–	–
,0	76,8	–	–	–

-6	1950	1960	1970	1973	1980
,7	3 279	3 591	3 888	3 973	4 100
,8		32,1		44,8	

Government and Parliament and the Supreme Court. The country's leading industrial city and most important commercial and shipping town.

Bergen (pop. 213,400). Norway's second largest city, is an old shipping and trading city and the cultural centre of Western Norway. *International Summer Festival* in May/June.

Trondheim (pop. 134,900). Important centre of trade, industry and shipping. The cathedral *Nidarosdomen* is the national shrine of Norway.

Stavanger (pop. 86,600) is the centre of the Norwegian fish-canning industry, and now also leads in shipbuilding. The Cathedral dates back to 1125.

Kristiansand (pop. 59,400). The "capital" of the south coast and centre of industry, trade and shipping.

Drammen (pop. 50,700). Administration centre for Buskerud county. Next to Oslo and Sarpsborg, Nor-

way's biggest export point for timberproducts.

Skien (pop. 47,100). Trade centre of Telemark county. Birthplace of Henrik Ibsen, the famous Norwegian playwright and poet.

Tromsø (pop. 43,800). Covers bigger area than any other Norwegian town. A port of departure for several great Arctic expeditions. Seat of northernmost university in the world, now being established.

Ålesund (pop. 40,800). Norway's largest fishing port with a large fishing fleet and a number of processing plants.

Government

The Constitution

The present Constitution of Norway was drafted by the National Assembly at Eidsvoll and proclaimed on 17th May 1814. Amendments were added subsequently. Influenced by British political tradition, the Constitution of the United States of America and the French Revolution ideas, the Norwegian Constitution is built on the sovereignty of the people.

The Constitution lays down that «The Kingdom of Norway is a free, independent, indivisible and inalienable realm. Its form of Government is a limited and hereditary monarchy." "The Evangelical Lutheran religion is the established religion of the country."

The most important provisions of the Constitution include the following: No-one may be convicted except by due process of law, or punished without trial. There shall be freedom of Press. Everyone shall be free to speak his mind frankly on the administration of the State, or on any other subject. No law may be given retroactive effect.

An age-old tradition guarding

King Olav V   Crown Prince Harald

family ownership of farm land secures the right of inheritance for the eldest child and entitles the family – within 5 years – to repurchase at a fair price any part of the family property which may have been alienated.

Under the Constitution, powers are divided between the King (and his Council, i.e. the Government), Parliament (Stortinget), and the Supreme Court of Justice.

The King

According to the Constitution, the executive power is exercised by the King-in-Council (King presiding over Cabinet). In exercising his constitutional powers the King is bound by majority decisions of the Cabinet. Under the Constitution, the King's selection of Cabinet members is subject to approval by Storting.

The King can use his right of veto to suspend legislation, he is the supreme commander of the country's armed forces, and he is the Head of the Church of Norway, to which he himself and at least half of his Cabinet must belong. In law, the King can do no wrong. He cannot be censored or indicted. The throne is hereditary, succession being in direct male descending line.

The Royal Family

H. M. King Olav V was born 2 July 1903, in England, the only son of

then Prince Carl of Denmark and Princess Maud of Great Britain. Married 1929 to Princess Märtha of Sweden († 1954), and succeeded his father King Haakon, on the death of the latter in 1957.

H. R. H. Crown Prince Harald was born in 1937, the third child and only son of the then Crown Prince Olav. The King and the Crown Prince both studied at Oxford, and both graduated from the Norwegian Military Academy.

In 1968, Crown Prince Harald was married to Miss Sonja Haraldsen (b. 1937) who gave birth to Princess Märtha Louise in 1971 and Prince Haakon Magnus in 1973.

The Princesses Ragnhild (b. 1930) and Astrid (b. 1932) are both married to Norwegian citizens.

Parliament

The Norwegian representative assembly or Parliament is called the Storting and is composed of 155 members. The Storting is elected for a term of 4 years, and cannot be dissolved in that period.

Constitutional and budgetary control is the responsibility of the Odelsting, which consists of 116 members of the Storting. Bills on legislation are presented to the Odelsting and have to be approved by the Lagting, which consists of 39 members of the Storting. Norway thus has a modified single house system.

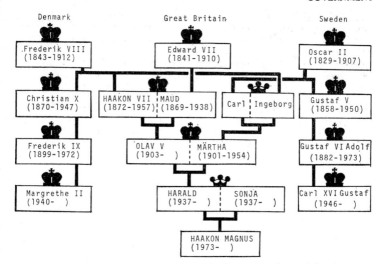

Interrelationship between the Norwegian and other European royal families.

The members of the Lagting may also, together with the Supreme Court, form the High Court of the Realm, to hear cases against members of the Government which may be raised by the Odelsting.

The Storting makes decisions on budgetary matters in plenary sessions. Every member is also member of one of the committees of the Storting. No report will be discussed in the Storting before it has been dealt with in one of the committees.

Election to Storting is by secret ballot, and elections take place on the same day in all electoral districts. Each county elects from four to fifteen representatives. Eligible for election are all men and women who in the year of election, have reached the age of 20 years and fulfill certain other requirements.

Representatives are elected by direct election in the individual districts which are entitled to a certain number of representatives, and on the basis of proportional representation.

In accordance with the will of Alfred Nobel, the Parliament elects a special committee awarding the Nobel Peace Prize. The Prize is awarded at a ceremony held in Oslo.

Universal Suffrage

All Norwegian subjects have the right to vote, provided they live in Norway on the day of voting and have not had their right of voting suspended or annulled. Norwegian subjects abroad may vote on certain conditions. Universal suffrage for men was introduced in 1898. Women received the right to vote in municipal elections from 1910 and in elections to Parliament from 1913. USA and Iceland were earlier than Norway in giving women the right to vote in municipal elections, but Norway was a pioneer in making women eligible for election to the national assembly. The first woman was elected to Parliament in 1911. At present (1973–1977) there are 24 women Members of Parliament.

Prior to 1920 voting age was 25, from 1920 till 1946 it was 23, and was then lowered to 21 and later 20 years of age.

11

The Political Parties

The Labour Party *(Det norske Arbeiderparti)* 1973 election – 759,499 votes, 35.3 %, 62 representatives in Parliament. Founded in 1887 to introduce socialism by democratic processes. Advocates a modern, moderate socialism and maintains close contact with social democratic parties of other countries.

Socialist Left Party *(Sosialistisk venstreparti)* 1973 election – 241,851 votes, 11,2 %, 16 representatives in Parliament. Founded in 1975. Originally formed as an electoral league in 1973 by The Socialist People's Party (Sosialistisk Folkeparti, SF), The Communist Party (Norges Kommunistiske Parti, NKP) and Democratic Socialists – AIK (Demokratiske sosialister – AIK). The league was transformed into a party in 1975. NKP continues as a party, but has no representatives in Parliament.

The Conservative Party *(Høyre)* 1973 election – 370,370 votes, 17.2 %, 29 representatives in Parliament. Founded in 1885, with the platform of "a sound conservative policy, upholding democracy, the right to property, and personal freedom". Advocates a modern progressive conservatism.

The Centre Party *(Senterpartiet)* 1973 election – 237,073 votes, 11.0 %, 21 representatives in Parliament. Founded in 1920 to promote the interest of the farming community. Now aims at attracting voters also from other sectors.

The Christian Democratic Party *(Kristelig Folkeparti)* 1973 election – 255,456 votes, 11.9 %, 20 representatives in Parliament. Formed as national party in 1938 to promote Christianity as basis of political life.

The Liberal Party *(Venstre)* 1973 election – 49,668 votes, 2.3 %, 2 representatives in Parliament. Founded in 1884 as a reform party. In 1972 the controversy whether Norway should join the Common Market or not, led to a split in the party, and The New Liberal Party was established.

The New Liberal Party *(Det Nye Folkepartiet)* 1973 election – 73,854 votes, 3.4 %, 1 representative in Parliament. Founded in 1972. (See above).

Anders Lange's Party for a Substantial Reduction of Taxes, Duties and Government Intervention *(Anders Langes Parti til sterk nedsettelse av skatter, avgifter og offentlige inngrep)* 1973 election – 107,784 votes, 5.0 %, 4 representatives in Parliament. Founded in 1973 as a protest party against growing state activity and the increasing burden of taxes and duties.

The Cabinet

The Norwegian Storting (Parliament did not become sovereign until 1884, subsequent to a conflict between the

The Parliament building (Stortinget) is centrally located in Oslo.

Composition of Parliament 1953—1973

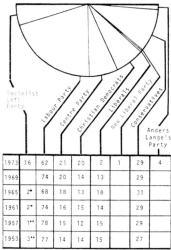

		Labour Party	Centre Party	Christian Democrats	Liberals	New Liberal Party	Conservatives	Anders Lange's Party
1973	16	62	21	20	2	1	29	4
1969		74	20	14	13		29	
1965	2*	68	18	13	18		31	
1961	2*	74	16	15	14		29	
1957	1**	78	15	12	15		29	
1953	3**	77	14	14	15		27	

* The Socialist People's Party
** The Communist Party

King (Oscar II of Sweden and Norway) and the Norwegian Government of Johan Sverdrup, the leader of the Liberal party. Formally, the Constitution empowers the King to appoint his Ministers: however, in practice it is the leader of the victorious party or parties who advises the King on the appointments to be made. The Prime Minister-Elect submits his ministerial list to the King for formal approval. Prior to World War II, the Storting dismissed minority governments on several occasions, and at times, the Storting also rejected Cabinet decisions, forcing the minister to resign. The Cabinet consists (1976) of the Prime Minister and 15 members.

Administration

Norway is administered under a system of central government and a system of local government. The country is divided into 19 counties (fylker), containing a total of 47 municipalities (bykommuner) and 396 rural districts (landskommuner), see inside of front cover.

Central administration

All important matters of administration are decided by the King-in-Council. Decisions are signed by the King and countersigned by the Prime Minister or the Cabinet Minister who has introduced the Bill. Constitutional responsibilities rest with the Cabinet, not with the King. Although the King-in-Council (the Government) may conclude treaties, treaties of major importance or treaties subject to new legislation do not become binding until approved by the Storting.

The Ministries

Authority to decide matters of minor importance is delegated to the various Ministers, in their capacity of Heads of Departments. Administrative authority is to a considerable extent delegated to subordinate bodies such as the Price Directorate (Prisdirektoratet), the Directorate for Customs and Special Tariffs (Direktoratet for Toll og Særavgifter), the Directorate of Public Health (Helsedirektoratet), etc.

Departments of State: Foreign Affairs, Trade and Shipping, Communications, Defence, Local Government and Labour, Fisheries, Industry, Finance and Customs, Church and Education, Agriculture, Social Affairs, Justice and Police, Environment, and Consumer Affairs and Government Administration.

The Ombudsman

Under legislation passed in 1962, a special "watch dog", the Ombudsman, (a commissioner) was appointed by Parliament to guard the rights of the citizen. The Ombudsman's field of work had previously been limited to the armed forces, but now includes also ombudsmen for civilian matters and consumer affairs.

Local Administration

Local government is administered by officials such as county governors, commissioners of police and sheriffs, and by publicly elected county, urban, and rural authorities.

Local self-government was instituted by an Act of 1837, as subsequently amended.

Norwegians pay taxes on income, capital, and other property to both the central government and to the local authority. Projects may be financed jointly or separately by the government, the counties and municipalities. The municipalities also pay taxes to the respective counties.

A tax reform, introduced 1970, reduced income tax and increased Value Added Tax.

Urban and Rural Municipalities

The urban and rural municipalities are governed by the *municipal councils* which have from 13 to 85 members, These councils are elected, on party-political lines, every 4th year. All citizens reaching the age of 20 during the year of election have the vote. Each council elects an Executive Board (Formannskap), consisting of one fourth of its members. In the major municipalities there are also councillors (paid officials) to handle the current business of the municipality.

Within the limits of the Local Government Act, the local authorities have fairly wide powers. They are responsible for elementary education, fire services, social security etc., and also for roads and highways.

Much of the money spent by local authorities comes by way of grants-in-aid from the central government, especially in the case of the less wealthy local authorities. Central government supervision is exercised by the relevant ministries, and also by the agency of the Fylkesmann (County Governor), particularly as regards matters concerning the economy, legal matters, education, and social policy.

In 1946 a Royal Commission was appointed to reorganize the system of local government. Many of the 680 rural districts and 64 urban districts were too weak financially to be capable of further development. By divisions and mergers the number of urban districts has been reduced to 47, that of rural districts to 396.

Counties (Fylker)

The counties are made up of the urban and rural districts within their boundaries. Each county is governed by a County Council (Fylkesting) consisting of representatives of the urban and rural districts. The County Council (fylkesting) elects a smaller body, the Fylkesutvalg (County Committee), which deals with day-to-day policy questions. The Fylkes-

The three latest Prime Ministers: From the left: Lars Korvald (1972–1973), Trygve Bratteli (1973–1976), Odvar Nordli (1976–).

The Government administration building in Oslo. Walldecorations by Picasso.

mann (County Governor) who is an official appointed by the King, is the chief civil administration authority of the county.

The responsibilities of the County authorities include the construction of roads and highways, hospitals, and secondary schools. The County Councils also cooperate in joint projects in the economic, social, and cultural fields. The County authorities collect taxes, and administer the revenue. The taxes are levied on the urban and rural district authorities.

Post War Politics

In order to effectively tackle the tremendous post-war reconstruction problems, all political parties agreed at the end of World War II on a joint post-war programme, when a coalition government was formed with *Einar Gerhardsen* as Prime Minister. Elections the same year gave Labour a majority in Parliament, with the support of a strong Communist group, and a pure Labour government was formed. War devastation and years of economic stagnation, together with the gradual abolition of numerous restrictions and control measures imposed by the Germans, faced the country with gigantic tasks of reconstruction and rehabilitation.

In 1949 Parliament elections the Labour Party achieved the greatest majority it had ever had, with 85 of 150 seats, while Communists lost all theirs. Post-war development in the East Bloc countries strongly influenced Norwegian policy, and was the most weighty of the factors in the Norwegian decision to join NATO. This decision, which was approved by Storting (Parliament) with a majority of 130 votes to 13, was made prior to the 1949 election.

An amendment of the electoral law reduced the Labour majority in the Parliamentary election of 1949.

In 1961 a dissenting party on the socialist wing, the Socialist People's Party, appeared on the political scene. This party directed its efforts mainly against the foreign and defence policies. The election gave the Socialist People's Party 2 representatives, Labour 74, and the four non-socialist parties 74. This situation was a great incentive towards closer cooperation between the non-socialist parties.

Changing Government

The post-war Labour Party epoch came to an end in 1963 and the four non-socialist parties formed a coalition government, which was, however, replaced by a new Labour government one month later. Having won the election in 1965, the four parties formed a coalition government (Prime Minister: Per Borten, Centre Party), with six cabinet ministers from the Conservatives and three from each of the other parties.

In the 1965–69-period the coalition parties had 80 seats in the Storting as against 70 opposition seats (Labour 68, Socialists People's Party (SPP) 2). The coalition parties renewed their

15

mandate in the 1969-election, but the majority in Stortinget was reduced to 76–74 (SPP disappeared).

Disagreement between the four parties caused a break in the coalition in February 1971. A Labour minority government was formed with Trygve Bratteli as Prime Minister. The Labour government resigned in September 1972 as a result af the referendum on EC and was followed by a three-party minority government (Centre Party, Liberal Party and Christian Democratic Party) led by Lars Korvald (Christian Democratic Party). The Liberal Party split after the referendum and a new party, The New Liberal Party, was established. The Norwegian Communist Party, the Sosialist People's Party, and a dissenting group from the Labour Party and independents concluded an alliance in 1973, before the election of Parliament.

A new Labour minority government – again led by Trygve Bratteli – was formed in October 1973, following general election in September. The two socialist-parties has 78 seats in the Storting, the nonsocialist parties 77 seats.

Economic Policy

Economic policy has been the major issue in post-war politics, with marked dissent on the questions of taxation and the degree of state interference in private trade and industry. Controls and restrictions found necessary by Labour led to bitter political strife on several occasions. A certain degree of planned economy was introduced, and some state-owned industrial enterprises were established. Also educational policy has been a controversial issue. On the other hand there has been substantial agreement on foreign and defence policies, and on measures to avoid detrimental labour conflicts. A number of strikes were avoided, because the Labour Relations Law contains a provision on compulsory arbitration. All parties cooperated in passing major social welfare legislation, e.g. the National Insurance Act of 1967 (see page 51).

International Relations

Norway fully supports international cooperation and the peaceful settlement of international conflicts. This is traditionally one of the main features of Norwegian foreign policy.

United Nations

Norway is one of the founder members of the UN and the then Norwegian Foreign Minister, Mr. Trygve Lie, became the first Secretary General of the world organization. Participation in the UN is a cornerstone of Norwegian foreign policy. Loyalty to the UN and fulfilment of obligations under the Charter are priorities in Norwegian foreign policy. Norway has always supported improvements to the peace-keeping ability of the UN, and has also actively supported measures to strengthen the influence and power of UN in international affairs.

Development Assistance

Norwegian assistance to developing countries has been made available through international organizations and bilateral schemes, with emphasis on technical assistance. A special Directorate under the Ministry for Foreign Affairs – NORAD – is responsible for the administration of the public assistance, which will reach the equivalent of 1 % of GDP by 1978. The figure for 1976 is Nkr 1,275 million.

National Security

In 1945 Norway saw the newly established United Nations as an instrument for collective security, but was soon disappointed in this respect. Later Norway took part in inconclusive discussions with a view to establishing a Scandinavian Defence Union and then became engaged in the preparations for Western collective self defence. Norway signed the North Atlantic treaty in 1949 and has since then been a member of NATO. Norway does not permit the stationing of foreign troops or nuclear weapons on Norwegian soil in peace time. By international agreement the archipelago of Svalbard (including the islands of Spitsbergen and Bjørnøya) is a demilitarised area.

The present defence policy meets with the support of the large majority in the Storting.

Western European Cooperation

Norway has been a member of the Council of Europe since the Council was established in 1949 and supports the idea of close European cooperation. In 1959 Norway played a leading role in establishing the European Free Trade association (EFTA). Norway has also been an active member of the Organization of Economic European Cooperation (OEEC) and its successor – the OECD, which in recent years has taken on increased importance. In 1972 the Norwegian Government concluded negotiations on membership in the EC, but in a referendum in September 1972 a majority voted against such membership. Negotiations were then initiated with a view to obtaining a trade agreement, which was signed in June 1973.

The Nordic Community

Common economic and social interests as well as a great many cultural and linguistic ties provide an atmosphere for easy communication between the Scandinavian countries. Although in 1949 the countries took different courses in their security policy, they have continued to work together closely in all other fields. One of the principal instruments of cooperation is the Nordic Council, set up in 1952 and consisting of parliamentarians from each of the member states (Denmark, Finland, Iceland, Norway and Sweden). Cabinet ministers also attend the Council sessions.

In 1973 a Nordic Council of Ministers was established as a permanent instrument for cooperation between the governments.

Justice

The country is divided into 5 *appelate court districts*, there being a total of 101 *primary court districts*, and 444 *conciliation board districts*.

The Supreme Court

The Supreme Court *(Høyesterett)* is seated in Oslo. It has one President and normally 17 permanent judges. Each case is heard by a bench of 5 judges. Because of the great influence which Supreme Court decisions have on legal practice, the rule is that if two (or more) give judgments which do not follow the precedent of previous Supreme Court decisions, then the case shall be decided by the court in plenary session. This rule also applies in certain other cases.

Proceedings are oral, but all evidence is written and presented by the barristers. The Judicial Select Appeals Committee of the Supreme Court *(Høyesteretts kjæremålsutvalg)* which consists of three Supreme Court judges decides on whether appeal from a lower court shall be allowed.

High Courts

Court of Appeals *(Lagmannsrett)* are found in 5 districts. The proceedings are conducted by a presiding judge with two other professional judges sitting together. In some civil cases two or four lay assessors (domsmenn) take part in the decision. In criminal cases the question of guilt is decided by a lay jury consisting of 10 persons, while the sentence is decided by the three professional judges. All proceedings are oral.

Primary Courts

In *Primary Courts* criminal cases are usually heard before one professional judge sitting with two lay assessors. In most civil cases the judge makes the decision unassisted. Proceedings are oral.

Conciliation Councils *(Forliksråd)* are found in all urban and rural districts. They each consist of three members, elected by the local administration for a period of four years. These councils mainly act as mediators to obtain amicable settlement between the parties out of Court, and under certain conditions

they also act as courts proper. All proceedings are oral and the parties meet without their lawyers.

Prosecution and Police

The prosecuting authorities are headed by the Director of Public Prosecutions and 14 district public prosecutors. In all cases of custody and in serious cases the counsel for the defence is paid by the State.

A special feature of the Norwegian police organization is that it combines the duties of a prosecuting agency with the general police activities. The police law officers may also by summary decisions impose fines, with the alternative of imprisonment. If the delinquent refuses to accept the fine, the case will be brought before the Court. The majority of such cases are settled out of Court.

The police is subordinate to the Minister of Justice and Police. The State pays all police expenses, a substantial part of which is refunded by the municipalities.

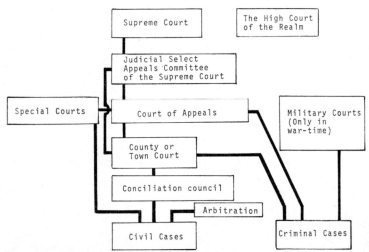

The principal features of the Norwegian legal system.

Defence

The general aim of Norwegian security policy is to preserve the freedom and security of Norway and at the same time to contribute to a peaceful development in other parts of the world. To reach this goal the security policy is based on two essential factors: a) Keeping up an adequate nation defence within the framework of the North Atlantic Treaty Organization of which Norway is a member. b) Making a continous political effort to contribute to the development of a detente and of mutual confidence between East and West.

The role of Norway's military defence has been defined as follows:

1. The Norwegian forces should contribute to the preservation of peace in our part of the world by:
   - maintaining an efficient surveillance and warning system.
   - maintaining the sovereignty of Norwegian territory, being able promptly to deter, limit or fight down various kinds of violations.
   - being able rapidly to reinforce the state of readiness in exposed areas, with the appropriate means.
   - being able to offer the strongest possible resistance against every form of attack.
   - preparing, in the best way possible, facilities for the reception of allied reinforcements.
2. The Norwegian defence forces should be prepared to give support to the peace-keeping mission of the United Nations, i.e. by assigning Norwegian contigents.
3. To the extent the above mentioned tasks permit, the defence forces should render as much assistance as possible to society as a whole.

Except for air defence forces, which are integrated in the NATO air defence system, Norway's forces are under national command in peacetime.

They will all, in war, or when the government so decides, be transferred to allied command. The C-in-C, Allied Forces Northern Europe, has his headquarters at Kolsås near Oslo. Foreign troops may at no time, except in time of war or immediate threat of war, be stationed on Norwegian soil, and it has been decided not to have nuclear weapons stationed in Norway.

Norway's strategic position is of prime importance. This particularly applies to the northern part of the country, the defence of which has therefore been given priority. The country has 122 miles of common border with the Soviet Union.

The Army

The largest operative unit of the Army is a combined regiment which numbers about 5,000 officers and men. Modern helicopters as well as pack horses are used for transportation purposes. Skis are part of the soldiers' equipment. New weapons and equipment include the AG-3 rifles, Leopard medium tanks, Armoured Personnel Carriers, 155 mm self-propelled artillery and snow vehicles of Swedish design. The *Home Guard*, consisting predominantly of military units of conscripts and also an element of volunteers is organized as local units which can be rapidly mobilized in case of war.

Naval Defence

Naval defence comprises the Royal Norwegian Navy and the Coastal Artillery. It is based on a coastal defence system. The Navy consists of smaller vessels, the largest being frigates of 1,800 tons. Others are patrol vessels, submarines specifically designed for Norwegian waters, torpedo boats and fast gun boats, landing craft and other small vessels.

Air Defence

Air defence includes the Air Force and the AA forces, which i.a. operate «Nike Hercules» rocket batteries. The Air Force is equipped with jet fighters and fighter bombers (Starfighters and Freedom fighters) with a varied weapon capability. The Air Force also operates a number of P 3 Orion Maritime patrol aircraft on surveillance duty over large sea areas and round the coast.

Military air transport capacity has been substantially increased by the introduction of C-130 «Hercules» transport aircraft.

Thus Army units may be moved over long distances in a matter of hours, giving mobility and flexibility to the defence of the country. For NATO infrastructure funds a control and warning system has been built for continuous radar surveillance of Norwegian air territory. The aircontrol and Early warning system is being further improved through the implementation of the so-called NADGE plan.

Conscription

Military service is compulsory for all male Norwegians from the age of 20 until 44. The length of service is 12–15 months with refresher training.

Finances

The Public Sector

Central and local government gross taxes in 1974 are estimated to absorb about 58,500 mill. kroner (nearly 46 % of the gross national product). During the sixties this percentage has increased from about 30 till about 41 in 1970. The percentage reached 45 in 1971. In 1939 less than 20 % of the GDP was absorbed by the public sector.

A characteristic feature of the development is the particularly large increase in government expenditure which may be described as transfers of income. In 1973 it was estimated that about 50 % of the revenue would be returned to the private sector in the form of price subsidies and other subsidies to trade and industry, social insurance benefits, and interest on government debt. The equivalent transfers in 1939 totalled about 25 % of the national revenue.

The National Fiscal Account, 1974 and 1975. Mill. kroner

Revenue	1974	1975	Expenditure	1974	1975
Property and income taxes . . . . . ·	5,757	5,986	Adm., courts and police	2,004	2,295
Customs duties	351	375	Defence	3,960	4,762
Value added tax	13,461	15,694	Education	4,337	5,043
Excise duties	6,167	7,179	Social services	4,624	5,298
Miscellaneous	4,563	5,247	Subsidies	1,231	1,321
			Communications	5,045	5,882
			Interests	1,688	1,956
			Development aid . . .	654	873
			Miscellaneous	5,445	8,104
Total		30,299 34,481	Total	29,988	35,474

Municipal Budgets

Total municipal revenues, which in 1974 were estimated at 20,100 mill. kroner, are mainly derived from taxes on income and property. In addition the municipalities receive substantial subsidies from the government. The system of allocation of subsidies aims at levelling the economies of the individual municipalities. Municipal budget expenditure is dominated by appropriations for education, social security and roads.

Debt

At the end of 1974 the central government debt totalled 33,943 mill. kroner, 3 per cent of which originated from foreign loans. At the end of 1973 the municipal loan debt totalled abt. 16,500 mill. kroner, about half of it connected with development of hydroelectric power.

Taxes

Income taxes are levied on assessed net income and paid to the central government and the municipalities by individuals and corporations.

Personal income tax to the central government was for 1975 levied at the following rates:

Tax rates per cent			Single person kr.	Families kr.
0	of the	first	20,000	30,000
6	of the	next	10,000	15,000
11	»	»	15,000	15,000
16	»	»	10,000	10,000
22	»	»	10,000	10,000
28	»	»	10,000	10,000
33	»	»	20,000	20,000
38	»	»	30,000	30,000
42	»	»	50,000	50,000
46	»	»	100,000	100,000
48	» exceeding income			

The rates of tax payable on income to the municipality may differ in the various municipalities. The maximum rate of which is applied by most municipalities is 21.3 per cent in 1975. The first 5,000 kroner of the net income of single tax payers and 10,000 kroner of families are tax-free.

A municipal tax is levied on the same tax base as the municipal tax.

The table below shows total income taxes, (including premiums for the National Insurance Scheme), as percentages of net income for single persons and for families (1975).

Net income kr.	Single persons	Families
20 000........	21,5 %	3,6 %
30 000........	25,8 %	12,5 %
40 000........	29,7 %	18,4 %
50 000........	32,5 %	22,5 %
100 000........	45,8 %	37,5 %

A municipal property tax is assessed on the basis of net value, i.e. gross property at assessed sales value with debts deducted. Bank deposits, shares, surrender value of life insurance policies, and personal possessions are taxed only in the event of their value exceeding certain stipulated limits. The individual net worth tax is levied at a rate of 1 per cent on net worth exceeding kr. 40,000.

Corporations pay to the central government a tax of 26.5 per cent (1975) of net income less dividends distributed by the corporations. In addition, corporations pay municipal income tax, (21,3 per cent) and municipal equalization tax (1,7 per cent).

In addition to income taxes several indirect taxes of different types are main sources of government revenues. The most important indirect tax is a general sales tax levied on a value added base at a rate of 20 per cent. Most commodities are effected. On the other hand prices on certain commodities, especially foods, are subsidized by the government, and in some cases these subsidies may offset the tax.

The Banks
The Bank of Norway

is formally organized as a corporation, but is owned by the government. It carries out the normal functions of a central bank and is only to a minor extent engaged in ordinary bank activities. The Bank of Norway has great influence on the planning and implementation of the country's monetary and credit policy. The Bank of Norway is the only bank in Norway entitled to issue bank notes.

The State Banks

are directly under government control. They were founded for the purposes of providing sources for supplementing private lending for social activities or for the promotion of trade and industry when this is found appropriate by the government. The Postal Giro and the Post Office Savings Bank finance their activities through deposits, while the other state banks finance their activities through loans and grants from the government and bearer bonds guaranteed by the government.

The Savings Banks

have old traditions in Norway. The first savings bank was founded in 1822. The savings banks, which numbered 411 at the end of 1974, are found all over the country. At the end of 1974 they administrated a capital of 29,700 mill. kroner. The banks play an important role in administrating the money of the small savers. Of the nearly 4,7 mill. deposit accounts (1973), only 15,000 involve amounts exceeding 100,000 kroner. The savings banks are also engaged in ordinary bank activities and meet a substantial part of local credit requirements. 1/3 of the credits consist of mortage loans.

The Commercial Banks

administrated at the end of 1974 a capital totalling 40,150 mill. kroner. Shortly before World War II there were more than 100 banks, but due to amalgamations the present number is 31. The three largest banks,

(Den norske Creditbank, Bergen Bank, and Christiania Bank & Kreditkasse) administrate more than 50 % of the total capital.

The commercial banks play a very important part as a service organ for trade and industry, not only by providing loans but also by offering a wide range of other services. The close relationship with trade and industry is reflected by the forms for loans and deposits. About 30 % of the loans are granted as current drawings accounts while about 20 % of deposits are at call.

Credit Market

Loans to private and municipal sectors from state and private banks, loan associations and insurance companies aggregated about 102,000 million kroner at the end of 1974. About 45 % of these loans were provided by incorporated banks and savings banks. Private and municipal sectors have in the recent years received an infusion of about 10,000 mill. kroner loan from Norwegian credit institutions. In 1974 the increase in loans amounted to 11,300. About 40 per cent of these loans were allocated to housing and commercial buildings.

By the end of 1974 the bearer bond debt in Norwegian kroner aggregated about 38,800 million kroner. A major part of this refers to government and municipality bonds. Private trade and industry bond debt in Norwegian kroner totalled 2,000 million kroner.

In addition to the loans provided by domestic credit institutions come borrowings by trade and industry abroad. By the end of 1972 foreign loans to trade and industry aggregated about 19,300 million kroner, bearer bond loans of 300 million kroner included.

In recent years monetary policy has been based mainly on regulations concerning liquidity reserve requirements. From October 1969 minimum investments in bearer bonds were made obligatory for banks and insurance companies in order to allocate capital to house building and other investments of high priority. Two new bodies were set up in 1970 to facilitate the cooperation between the authorities and the credit institutions.

Insurance

There are 12 life insurance companies and 120 companies which are engaged in other branches of insurance. Premiums paid to Norwegian companies in 1973 totalled about 3,600 mill. kroner.

The activities of the insurance companies are governed by Statute. Legislation particularly aims at protecting the insured. Permission to engage in insurance business is subject to government concession, approval of the insurance conditions, and that assets be placed in safe investments. In practice, most of the assets are invested in mortgages and in bearer bonds.

Economy

General Survey

The economy of Norway is based on agriculture, forestry, fishing, shipping, hydroelectric power production and the manufacturing industries based thereon. Foreign trade is essential to the economy, and the merchant fleet is one of the main sources of financing Norway's continuing import surplus.

The expansion of industry in the 20th century is primarily based on the country's cheap waterpower, but also on a better utilization of the natural resources, such as fish, timber, ores and metals.

The recent discovery of mineral oil in the North Sea will have a great influence to Norwegian economy in the near future.

Employment

Expressed in man-working years, employment in 1974 totalled about 1.6 mill. As appears from the table below, more than one third of employment was in manufacturing industry, mining, building and construction, power and water supply.

The groups commerce, transport and communications, administration and other services account for more than $1/2$ of total employment, agriculture, forestry and fishing for $1/10$.

Employment has increased slightly in the '50s and '60s, approximately with the same rate as the number of inhabitants. The numbers employed in the primary industries (agriculture, forestry, fishing) are falling, while on the other hand they have increased in commerce, in the educational and health services, and in other service industries.

Norway has a tight labour market with full employment. In a number of trades skilled labour is scarce. However, there is some seasonal unemployment, especially during the winter months and in the building and construction trades. This is because some types of work cannot be carried out during the cold season. Fishing, agriculture and forestry are also seasonal trades. The seasons do not altogether overlap, but despite this fact, a combination of employment in these trades and also in building and construction is common in Norway.

The Gross Domestic Product

The GDP increased from 15,018 mill. kroner in 1950 to 128,792 mill. kroner in 1974. In volume terms the increase was 238,5 %. Distribution of the GDP was in 1974 as follows in % :

Employment and GDP – Distribution by Trades %

	Employment		GDP	
	1950	1974	1950	1974
Agriculture	23,8	7,8	3,1	7,5
Forestry	2,2	0,6	1,1	2,6
Fisheries, whaling and sealing......	3,8	1,4	1,4	3,7
Manufacturing and mining........	24,2	24,9	23,8	27,5
Electricity and water supplies......	0,8	0,9	2,9	2,1
Building and construction.........	7,3	8,3	8,1	6,6
Trade	8,9	13,3	18,3	15,2
Water transport.................	3,9	3,3	8,4	11,1
Other transport and communic.	5,5	7,2	6,4	5,8
Public administration, armed forces and other services..............	19,6	32,3	26,5	17,9
	100,0	100,0	100,0	100,0

Consumer expenditure	52,3
Government expenditure ...	16,4
Investments	33,8
Exports	47,7
Total demand.............	150,2
Minus imports	50,2
GDP	100,0

Compared with other countries with which it is appropriate to draw comparisons, the *rate of investment* is exceptionally high. Nearly half of investments are in the building and construction sector, and the balance in machinery, ships and other transport facilities. About 50 % of Norwegian exports are goods and the rest gross freight earnings and other earnings in foreign currency and export of second-hand ships. Of imports about ¼ are ships and the operational expenses of the merchant fleet abroad. Total exports and imports amount to about 50 % of GDP. This clearly illustrates the significance of foreign trade to Norwegian economy.

The table at the top of this page shows the contributions of the various trades to the GDP in 1950 and 1974. Generally speaking, the figures show the same trend in Norwegian economy as do the equivalent figures for employment. *Forestry* and *fisheries* would seem to play a relatively modest role in the Norwegian economy, but it should be remembered that they form the basis for several of Norway's most important industries, which contribute a total of 20 % of the value of Norwegian industrial production and about 25 % in value of commodity exports.

Building and construction are more prominent in the Norwegian economy than in the economies of most of the other countries in Western Europe. Particularly after World War II major investments have been made in the development of hydro-electric power, in industries based on ample supplies of electric power, and in roads and housing.

Domestic sea and land *transport and communications* are of relatively great significance to Norwegian economy. Due to the length and topography of the country as well as the scattered population, building and maintenance of communications are exceedingly expensive. *Education and health services* weigh heavily on the country's budget. Compared with other countries on the same development level, employment in *administration* is not very high.

Agriculture

About 10 % of the total manyears in Norway were in 1972 carried out in agriculture.

Practically all farmers own their own farms. The aggregate agricultural

The farms are highly mechanized. This picture shows a forage harvester at work in Romsdalen, southern Norway.

acreage is about 2.4 million, equivalent to 3.0 % of the total land area, and there are 120,746 farms (1974) with more than 1.2 acres (0.5 ha), 34,231 fewer than in 1969.

The Farms

Farms are small. Only 60 have more than 250 acres (1972). 43,852 farmers have farming as their sole occupation, while 27,480 farmers have their farms as their main occupation and 56,289 farmers are part-time farmers with their main income sources outside agriculture. In the coastal area farming is often combined with fishing, while in the inland districts earnings are supplemented by working in the forests. Many farms have forests in addition to their farmland.

Due to the climatic conditions, the growing season is very short, and springtime work and harvesting thus become very labour intensive seasons, however, agriculture has difficulty in paying the same wages as industry and other trades. Hired labour, therefore, is scarce in agri-

culture. Almost 95 % of the work is done by the farmer himself and his family, but the farms are highly mechanized.

Agricultural Production

Norwegian agriculture is mainly based on livestock and on production of fodder. *Milk* is the main sales product, followed by *beef, pork, eggs,* and *poultry.* About 50 % of the milk production is processed to cheese and other milk products. Norway also has a comparatively large number of *sheep* with a large production of *wool.* To many farms *fur farming* is an important source of supplementary income (value of furs exceeds value of wool production).

About ⅓ of the agricultural area is crop and horticultural land, while ⅔ is meadow and grazing land. The main crops are *grain,* (almost entirely barley and oats), and *potatoes.* In some districts the *fruit* and *berry crops* are of great importance to local economy. Vegetables are produced near main consumer centres, where the

25

climate also is favourable, especially in the Oslo fjord area and Jæren. Sales value of market garden crops is greater than that of the grain crops.

Production and quality of animal products are dependent on imports of protein feeding stuffs. Norwegian-produced animal feeding stuffs have generally a high content of carbohydrates. Practically all bread grain is imported, as are all southern fruits. Some vegetables are also imported to supplement Norwegian production. Norwegian agriculture is being rapidly mechanized, adopting production forms with less demand for manpower. It can be mentioned that the number of holdings with cows 1959–1974 have been reduced from 150,000 to 53,865.

Norwegian farmers have their own selling and purchasing cooperatives which play an important role in Norwegian agriculture and agricultural policy. In order to fulfil the policy-aims of agriculture which are agreed upon by the Storting, government subsidizes are given to maintain a certain level of income in agriculture, to maintain a certain production level

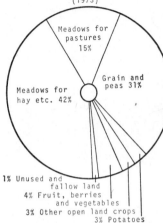

Total area approx. 2,23 mill. acres (1973)

Meadows for pastures 15%

Grain and peas 31%

Meadows for hay etc. 42%

1% Unused and fallow land
4% Fruit, berries and vegetables
3% Other open land crops
3% Potatoes

Utilization of cultivated agricultural area.

and to maintain settlements in remote areas.

Forestry

The export of lumber was from the 16th to the beginning of the 20th century one of Norways' main exports. This trade has, however, given way to products of the wood processing industries, which amount to about 12 % of total export.

The forests of Norway which are among the most northern in the world, cover about 19.8 million acres, or about $1/_5$ of the total land area. About 16.2 million acres are productive, the remainder being mountain forests. Of the productive forests 80 % are coniferous (mainly spruce). The total cubic content of the productive forests is about 14,100 mill. cu. feet, annual growth 477 mill. cu. feet, while about 300 mill. cu. feet are cut annually.

Ownership

About ⅔ of the forest area is owned by farmers. Some of this area lies in so-called «parish commons», jointly owned by the farmers using them. These forests vary

Fur farming is an important additional income for many Norwegian farmers.

in size from a few acres to severa sq. miles. Of the remaining ⅓ about one half is owned by the government and municipalities, the rest by industrial concerns, companies and other private enterprises.

Work in Forests

Work in the forests is being increasingly mechanized. Cutting is mostly done with motor saws, while tractors, trucks, funiculars and winchers are utilized in the transportation of logs. 30–35,000 miles of forest roads have been built for timber transport. Such roads are being extended by some 1,300 miles each

Farm machinery
per 1.000 acres farm land

4-wheeled tractors 46
2-wheeled tractors 8
Combine harvesters 6
Forage harvesters 12

* 20 per 1.000 acres grainland

Average annual yield per acre
in kg, (1973):

Grain 1319 Potatoes 9291 . Hay 2784

Average annual production
in kg, (1973):

Milk per cow 4520
Eggs per hen 10
Wool per sheep 6

Production of beef and pork totals
about 153 thousand tons.

year. The government supports construction of forest roads. Floating of timber in the rivers, formerly almost the only means of inland long-distance transport, is now being replaced by road and rail transport.

Forest Preservation

All forests, public as well as privately-owned are under government supervision, ensuring that good care is taken of the great resources which the forests represent in the national economy. On request, government forestry officers will give forest owners professional advice. A certain percentage of the income from sales of timber is allocated to forest rehabilitation funds. The government also subsidizes *planting of forests*. About 1 million acres are considered suitable for afforestation.

Annually 70–80,000 acres are planted with trees which will be ready for cutting in 50–100 years, depending on the quality of the soil and the dimensions desired.

Fisheries

The warm currents of the Gulf Stream which flow along the shores of Norway provide the basis for rich fishing grounds, with favourable growth conditions for considerable local stocks of many varieties of fish. The Norwegian fjords and coastal banks are also the spawning grounds for the great shoals of cod, herring and other fish species that come in from the northeastern areas of the Atlantic.

The Norwegian fisheries are thus predominantly based on the exploitation of fish stocks along the coast and the coastal banks. Norwegian deep-sea fisheries operating more than 200 nautical miles offshore or along the coasts of foreign countries account for about 20 per cent of the total national catch. Trawling is as a general rule prohibited within the fishery limit, thus leaving a major

27

part of the codfish catch to be taken by the gill net, long-line and hand line. Pelagic species are usually fished by purse seine.

Productivity and efficiency in the fishing industry have increased considerably during the last decade. There has been a transition to larger vessels, with more powerful engines, hydraulic hauling gear and electronic equipment for locating fish and for navigation. There has been an almost complete change-over from natural to artificial fibres for gear and tackle.

Fishing operations provide, wholly or in part, direct employment and income for approximately 4 per cent of the population of Norway. In the coastal districts, and particularly in the three northernmost counties, the percentage is far higher: in Finnmark 18 per cent, in Troms 16 per cent, and in Nordland 14 per cent. In addition, a large percentage of the population of these counties is employed in industries closely related to fishing, such as fish processing, the fish meal industry, boatbuilding and repair yards, gear manufacture, and the marketing and transport of fish products. Further south, fishing is of greatest relative importance in the county of Møre and Romsdal where, directly and indirectly, fishing provides the basis for the employment and income of at least one fifth of the county's population.

During the years 1970–1973 the average annual fish catch in Norway totalled 2.8 million tons, making Norway the fifth biggest fishing nation in the world (after Japan, the U.S.S.R, China and Peru). In 1974 the total catch of the Norwegian fisheries was 2.4 million tons, with a first-hand value of 2,200 million kroner. Species which are primarily used for meal and oil, in particular capelin, made up about 70 to 80 per cent of the total volume of the catch and about 40 per cent of the first-hand value. Cod, coalfish, haddock, etc., which are used mainly for human consumption, accounted for about 16 per cent of the catch and 44 per cent of the first-hand value. The remainder of the catch, approximately 4 per cent, consisted of other fish and shellfish, mostly for human consumption.

The fishing fleet and fishing methods

The Norwegian fishing fleet is characterized by the great number of small units. The fleet consists of about 27,000 vessels with engines, of which about 26,000 are boats up to 50 g.r.t., 370 vessels of 51–150 g.r.t., 425 vessels of 151–500 g.r.t., 54 vessels of 501–900 g.r.t. and 13 factory trawlers above 900 tons.

Recent Norwegian legislation enables the government to exercise an effective control over the development of the fishing fleet in accordance with the available stocks of fish. The fishermen have to obtain individual licences from the government in order to engage in the various types of fisheries.

The fishermen

In recent years there has been a considerable decline in the number of fishermen. The 1948 census showed a total of 86,000 fishermen; by 1960 the number had fallen to roughly 61,000, and in 1971 the total number was about 35,000. Of these, 16,000 have fishing as their sole occupation.

However, there are still many fishermen who combine fishing with another occupation, the most important combinations being fishing/farming and fishing/building (or construction work).

The fishermen are primerily paid by shares from the gross income of the vessel less certain joint expenses.

The fishermen are organized in the Norwegian Fishermen's Association. The owners of the fishing vessels are also members of this association.

Catch – Utilization – Value 1973

Species	Catch		Utilization in tons		Utilization – value in 1000 kr.	
	tons	firsthand value	consumption	bait, animals' feed, meal and oil	consumption	bait, animals' feed, meal and oil
Herring, mackerel, capelin	1.832.899	722.905	102.712	1.730.187	113.001	659.904
Cod, saithe, haddock ...	402.961	722.995	402.155	806	722.639	356
Tusk, ling..............	37.234	111.966	37.233	1	111.965	1
Norway tout, sandeel, polar cod etc.	194.836	74.210	—	194.836	—	74.210
Spur-dog	14.883	18.377	14.828	55	18.331	46
Greenland halibut	12.741	24.245	12.693	48	24.236	9
Deep water prawn	12.157	81.386	12.125	32	81.174	212
Others................	200.671	183.566	25.867	174.804	103.850	79.716
TOTAL	2.708.382	1.989.650	607.613	2.100.769	1.175.196	814.454

Processing

The major part of the total Norwegian catch is processed in some form or another, with only about 3 per cent used as fresh fish.

The Norwegian processing industry consists of a large number of small plants scattered along the entire coast, along with a relatively small number of large units. About two-thirds of the processing plants are located in the three northernmost counties. The canned fish industry is primarily located in West Norway.

Most of the fish for human consumption was formerly used for the traditional production of stockfish, klipfish and salted fish. Considerable quantities of these products are still produced. Klipfish, which consists of salted and dried codfish, is produced chiefly in West and North Norway. In recent years, however, the freezing and filleting industry has undergone a rapid expansion, particularly in North Norway. A growing proportion of fish for human consumption is being processed into frozen fish products, particularly frozen fillets. The fluctuations in the supply of raw materials represents a serious problem to this industry, leading to difficulties in achieving full utilization of capacity at all times.

Frozen fillets and highly processed frozen fish products are now the major products of the Norwegian fishing industry. There are 236 freezing plants in Norway. Norway has 55 fish meal and fish oil plants which make use of 75 to 80 per cent of the total Norwegian catch, primarily consisting of species not generally used for human consumption. Norway has 13 factory freezer trawlers. Their production, primarily frozen fillets, is sold and delivered directly to buyers in foreign countries.

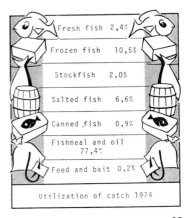

Fresh fish 2,4%
Frozen fish 10,5%
Stockfish 2,0%
Salted fish 6,6%
Canned fish 0,9%
Fishmeal and oil 77,4%
Feed and bait 0,2%

Utilization of catch 1974

Marketing and exports

All the fish landed in Norway is sold through the fishermen's own sales organisations. All persons or firms wishing to purchase fish for processing or resale must be approved by the respective sales organisation. The organisations vary in both structure and methods, but they have a common goal: to stabilise prices and to ensure that the fishermen receive the highest price that the market will permit.

At present there are 13 sales organisations with the sole right of first-hand sale. This right is either related to a specific geographic area or to a definite fish species or a combination of area and species.

Norway exports 85–80 per cent of the total catch. The value of the fish and fish products exported in 1974 amounted to 2,884 million kroner (excluding hardened fish fats with a value of 331 million kroner), and represented about 10 per cent of total Norwegian exports of commodities. The major categories of fish exports, with the percentage of the total, were as follows:

	Million N.kr.	%
Fish, fresh, chilled, frozen (excl. fillets)	203	7
Frozen fillets (incl. fish sticks, breaded portions, etc.)	600	21
Shellfish (incl. peeled prawns, frozen or in brine)	91	3
Fish, salted or dried, smoked..........	877	30
Fish oil (incl. fish liver oil)	107	4
Fish meal	673	23
Canned products ...	272	9
Other	61	2

Norwegian fish products are exported to most countries of the world, with the United Kingdom, the United States and Sweden representing the most important markets.

Of Norwegian exports of fish products in 1973, some 42 per cent went to the enlarged European Community, while the EFTA countries took 17 per cent and the U.S. 12 per cent.

In recent years Norwegian fishermen have been witnessing with increasing anxiety the trend towards an over-exploitation of the living resources of the sea. Important agreements have been reached within the regional Fisheries Commissions for the Northeast and Northwest Atlantic. Catch quotas have also been established through various multilateral and bilateral negotiations. It is nevertheless quite clear that the international agreements for safeguarding the living resources of the sea have thus far not been sufficiently effective. The Norwegian government is consequently in favour of strengthening the jurisdiction of the coastal states. In September 1974 the government declared that the necessary preparations would be started for extending the Norwegian fishery limit to 50 nautical miles and later to 200 nautical miles in accordance with the principles of international law. The Norwegian fishery limit has been 12 nautical miles since 1961.

Norway has a great export of frozen fish fillets.

Sealing

Norwegian sealing takes place in the Arctic Ocean, the North West Atlantic (Newfoundland) and also in the Barents Sea. In 1973 32 sealers carried home 115,200 fur skins and 2,054 tons of blubber at a total landing value of 16.6 mill. kroner. The participation in sealing has declined from 51 ships in 1966 to 32 ships in 1973.

Power Supply
Electricity

The total capacity of waterpower resources capable of economic development is estimated at 120,000 mill. kWh a year, about 58 per cent of which was harnessed by the end of 1974, when operational generator capacity totalled 16,072,000 kW. Hydro-electric power plants account for nearly 100 per cent of Norway's supply of electricity. The development of some of the waterpower resources, however, is dependent on relatively heavy investments per kWh produced which would make the projects unprofitable compared with other possibilities for producing the same amount of power. Out of regard for nature preservation, some waterfalls will not be harnessed.

Development and Consumption

Large-scale development of Norwegian waterpower resources was commenced around the turn of the century. Cheap waterpower was the basis of electro-chemical and electro-metallurgical industries, which at the beginning of World War I had gained international importance. Generator capacity increased from 550,000 kW in 1914 to 1,240,000 kW in 1930, when 68 per cent of the population were supplied with electricity. In 1945 generator capacity had reached 2,360,000 kW and an annual production of 10,000 mill. kWh.

After World War II demands for cheap electric power for new industries and heating of dwellings speeded up development. By the end of 1973 99.99 per cent of the population were supplied with electricity. The Norwegian per capita consumption of 17,890 kWh in 1974 is the highest in the world, and twice as much as that of Canada, Sweden and USA, which come next in international statistics.

About 45 per cent of the electricity production is consumed by the electro-chemical and electro-metallurgical industries, leaving the other industries with 18 and transport, households, agriculture and lighting the remaining 37 per cent, exclusive of electric boilers.

The Norwegian and the Swedish grid systems are connected. Regular exports of power from Norway to Sweden started in 1960–61, and amounted in 1974 to about 5,800 mill. kWh. On the other hand Sweden exports power from thermal power stations to Norway when Norwegian water magazines are low, but usually the import of power to Norway is less than one tenth of the export. There is also cooperation in development of the basins in Norway of rivers flowing into Sweden. Since 1970 Norway has also imported some power from the USSR, about 60 mill. kWh a year.

Future Development

During the period 1950–60 the average increase in production of hydro-electricity was 1,420 mill. kWh a year, equivalent to an annual increase in generator capacity of 350,000 kW. In 1960–70 production increased further by 3,500 mill. kWh annually, equivalent to 700,000 kW generator capacity. The long-term target is an annual increase of 3,200 mill. kWh or 650,000 kW generator capacity. It is estimated that Norway will have sufficient cheap waterpower until the middle of the 1980s when it will be necessary to provide supplementary power from other sources.

31

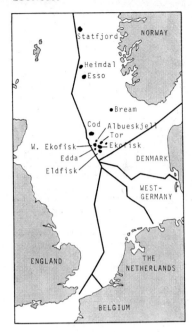

It is found economical to introduce some thermal power in the existing hydro-dominated power-system already in the 1970s in order to avoid the influence of "dry" years. This has been attained by signing contracts between the State Power Board in Norway (NVE) and various power-companies in Sweden and Denmark. The contracts grant Norway import of thermal power when it is most needed. The import from Denmark necessitates the laying of two 130 km long DC cables across the ocean of Skagerrak. The first cable is expected to be operating in 1976 and the next one in 1977.

Having harnessed the main part of the economically exploitable water-power, the question has arisen whether the further basic power production will be based on conventional thermal or nuclear power plants. The discovery of large deposits of gas and oil off the Norwegian coast will possibly be of great significance in this respect.

Oil and gas

The history of Norway's oil and gas development is short and dramatic. Norway declared her sovereignty over the Continental Shelf in 1963, detailed rules were enacted in 1965, and the first drilling on allocated blocks started in 1966.

The first years were disappointing, and interest was tapering off when the Phillips Group just before Christmas 1969 announced a big oil find in block 2/4. This find was subsequently named Ekofisk. It soon became evident that this was a major find, possibly among the 50 largest fields in the world.

The international oil industry renewed its interest in the North Sea, which is now one of the most prolific oil and gas areas in the world. About 25 discoveries have now been made on the Norwegian shelf, of which three to four areas can be considered viable for commercial development. The Ekofisk area (with eight to nine fields) is now on stream, with a production far exceeding the daily domestic demand in Norway. Hence, Norway is the only country in Western Europe to be a net exporter of oil. Eventually, the oil production from the Ekofisk complex will be around one million barrels a day, through a pipeline to Teesside in the UK. In addition, the area will produce about 20,000 million cubic metres of gas, through a pipeline to Emden in West Germany.

Other major areas are Frigg (the world's largest offshore gas field), now under development for production through a pipeline to Scotland in 1977, Heimdal (development still uncertain) and Statfjord. Statfjord is the world's fourth largest offshore oil and gas field, and by far the largest field in the North Sea. Production start probable in early 1978.

Proved, exploitable reserves are now about 850 million tons of oil and 800 000 million cubic metres of natural gas. As less than 10 per cent

The first of a series and a Norwegian innovation. A huge Condeep concrete platform for oil drilling, production and storage is here under tow from Stavanger to Mobil's Beryl field in the British sector of the North Sea.

of the Norwegian Shelf has been ecplored so far, it is still too early to predict the true magnitude of the eventual oil and gas reserves.

The Norwegian Continental Shelf is by far the largest in Europe. When the areas north of the 62nd parallel are included, it comprises 25 per cent of Europe's total shelf area. Since the Geneva Convention of 1958, which divided the North Sea according to the midline principle, only the area south of the 62nd parallel has ben open for exploration. The shelf boundaries in the Norwegian Sea and the Barents Sea are still to be determined. Negotiations concerning the Barents Sea shelf boundaries with the USSR, have been underway for the last couple of years.

However, the Norwegian Government has stated that oil exploration in a specific offshore area outside Troms should start in the summer of 1977.

Oil exports

It is already clear, however, that the oil development will have a significant impact on Norway and its economy. In 1975 oil production from the Ekofisk area alone surpassed domestic comsumption in Norway. Hence, Norway became a net exporter of oil, being the only Western country in this category.

The oil resources and exports will bring considerable revenues to the country. In 1978 it is estimated that the oil revenues will exceed Nkr 8,000 million (US $ 1,500 million) increasing to more than US $ 2,000 million in 1980.

This will enable Norway to repay her foreign debts and in the 1980s the country for the first time will become a capital exporting country.

It is the aim of the Norwegian Government to use the revenues in such a way as to benefit the country as a whole. The main point is not to use the revenues for a rapid development in certain industries, at the expense of the existing industrial base in Norway. Norway is a high cost country, and the use of the oil revenues could create unwanted inflationary strains on the economy.

Therefore, a sensible rate of development has been advocated. The

Norwegian Storting has suggested that an acceptable level of production would be 90 million tons of oil equivalents (oil and gas) annually. This level could be attained in the mid 1980s. With this rate of extraction, the oil development should not cause undue strains on the economy.

Another point has been to pre-empt some of the oil revenues in 1975 and 1976. This is done by borrowing money abroad and spending it to keep full employment. These loans can easily be repaid by the revenues in the period 1977–1980.

In addition to having a strict economic control of the development, it has been Norway's policy since 1969 that there should be an element of state participation in the development, mainly in order to acquire knowledge of a new industry. Hence, a state oil company, Statoil, was established by an unanimous vote in the Norwegian Storting in 1972. State participation is usually 50 per cent.

There is a close cooperation with international oil companies, and this cooperation is expected in the years to come.

The oil development has also given a boost to existing Norwegian industry. Large production platforms and storage tanks have been built in Norway, based on Norwegian design.

In fact, concrete production facilities have been pioneered by Norwegian firms. Furthermore, Norwegian firms have ownership interests in about 60 drilling rigs and over 100 supply ships, and the largest supply bases in Europe are in Stavanger, Norway. Rigs and production platforms have hitherto been mainly an American speciality. For the North Sea they are just as much a Norwegian speciality.

Mining and Quarrying

One of the oldest of the large mines was Kongsberg Silver Mine which was in operation from 1624 until 1957. Two other mines from the middle of the 17th century are still in operation, Røros and Løkken. Originally both mines were copper mines. Today zinc is the main product in Røros. In Løkken, pyrites was the main product for many years. Today however, the mine is again producing copper and in addition zinc as a by-product.

In Norway copper is mostly found together with pyrites. Today there are 11 mines producing about 100,000 tons copperconcentrates (about 20–30 % Cu) every year.

It was not until the middle of the 19th century, with the development

Hydro-electric power plants account for nearly 100 % of Norway's supply of electricity.

Manufacturing Industries in Norway

Principal figures for manufacturing industries 1972–1974

	1972	1973	1974
Establishments	13,559	13,679	14,372
Persons engaged	375,761	376,018	385,140
Gross value of production mill. kr.	60,046	69,060	88,350
Value added » »	20,764	23,907	28,682
Gross fixed capital formation » »	3,250	3,450	5,465

Establishments and persons engaged by type of ownership in mining, quarrying and manufacturing 1972–1974

	Establishments			Persons engaged		
	1972	1973	1974	1972	1973	1974
Individual	4,815	4,677	4,935	36,270	33,617	31,699
General partnership	2,300	2,398	2,326	24,801	24,128	22,185
Joint-stock companies, cooperatives and others.	6,948	7,168	7,574	324,175	327,849	345,956
Total	14,063	14,243	14,835	385,246	385,594	399,840

of the chemical industry and its demand for sulphur, that pyrites became valuable.

Cheap recovery of sulphur from crude oil has resulted in an excess supply of sulphur which in turn has made the traditional sulphur extraction less profitable.

Some years ago 6 pyrites mines were in operation. Today there are only 2 pyrites mines in operation.

Iron ore is mined at 5 mines. The ore contains 33–35 % iron, which is dressed to a concentrate containing about 65 % iron.

The two largest iron ore mines are Sydvaranger, near the Soviet border in Finnmark, and Rana, close to the Arctic Sircle. The former has a production of about 2,5 million tons (65 % Fe) per year, the latter about 1 million tons (62–70 % Fe) but here the target is a production comparable to that of Syd-Varanger.

The greatest deposit of ilmenite ore (ferrotitanium ore) in Europe is located in the southwestern part of the country (Sokndal), where there is a modern mining plant.

Some of the mines also produce lead- and zinkconcentrates as by-products.

In Spitzbergen Norway has one coal mine in operation, which provides supplies for a coking plant at Mo in Rana, Northern Norway.

A number of non-metallic minerals which are mined or quarried are of great value as raw material and subsidiary materials for other industries. Limestone is used for nitrate of lime, calcium carbide, cement and the smelting works. Quartz is used in the production of ferroalloys and magnesium, feltspat and nepheline-syenite for ceramics and glass.

For building and monumental stones there is quarrying of granite, marble, slate, larvikite and different other kinds of stone.

Manufacturing Industries

In our century there has been a great development within the Norwegian manufacturing industries. During the period 1960–72 the average annual increase in production has been about 5 per cent. Employment has increased very moderately, the higher production being mainly due to increased productivity.

The manufacturing industries today dominate Norwegian economy, and their share in the GNP and total employment is far greater than that of other branches of industry.

Structure of Industry

It has been common practice to distinguish between *export industries* and *domestic industries*, depending on the main markets for their produce. The distinction between the export and the domestic industries is however not so marked as previously, more and more branches of traditional domestic industries having successfully expanded their activities to foreign markets. This is particularly the case with the engineering industries.

Although the range of commodities in Norwegian exports is widening, most of the income from exports comes from the traditional *export industries*, the forest, the electro-metallurgical, the electro-chemical, and the fishing industries. Of the typical *domestic industries*, the most important are the iron and metal, the food and drink, and the textile and clothing industries.

Despite the manufacturing industries' prominent position in Norwegian economy, there is not the same type of concentration of industry in Norway as is common in other Western European countries.

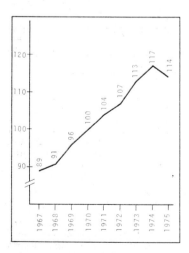

Index of Manufacturing production (value added), annual. 1970=100

The plants are located all over the country, but especially on the coast. The main concentration is in the Oslofjord area, with about half of the country's industry located in the surrounding counties. Other industrial locations include the coast as far north as Trondheim, with concentration around the major cities, while there is very little industry in northern Norway.

Typical Norwegian industrial plants are usually small. Plants engaged in export industries are generally larger than the plants manufacturing for the domestic market.

8,347 manufacturing enterprises have 5 or more employees. Of this group 283 enterprises have more than 200 employees.

Future of Industry

Partly because of the substantial public revenues from the petroleum sector, a rapid increase in domestic demand is expected. This will cause a slight decline in the industrial employment. Despite a rapid development of productivity, the growth will be less than in the 60-ies.

In the long run the target for industrial development is a change-over from a raw material orientated industry to a manufacturing industry. Such a transformation is a precondition for continued industrial growth.

It is assumed that the limitation of growth for the traditional export industries lies mainly in the production capacity, especially since the supply of raw materials and electric power will be limited.

Simultaneously the finds of oil and gas in the continental shelf have provided opportunities for a new industry geared towards these resources. In this connection the potentialities of development of petro-chemical industry are of topical interest. The activities on the continental shelf have also provided orders for the industry for deliveries of equipment for drilling and production. This will in particular give

Production of unwrought aluminium, primary, in 1973 totalled about 620,000 t.

growth opportunities to the engineering industry.

The Forest Industries

The forest industries have for several hundred years provided some of Norway's main exports. Today the lumber mills and the other wood industries work mainly for the home market, while the *pulp and paper industry* concentrates on the export market, the main products being *woodpulp* and *paper*.

The wood processing industries have traditionally been some of the most important export industries of Norway, but the importance has recently declined somewhat.

Electro-metallurgical Industries

The great electro-chemical and electro-metallurgical industries, require large supplies of power (45 % of the country's total production of electricity) and also easy access to international sea transport for their exports. Conditions in Norway are well suited for such production and there exists a comprehensive and well developed industry in these fields. Investments have after World War II been substantial and production in these fields has increased considerably more than in the manufacturing industries in general.

Production of *unwrought aluminium, primary*, in 1973 totalled about 620,000 tons, zinc 80,500 tons, nickel 42,700 tons, and copper 33,300 tons. Production of *ferro-alloys* is also very substantial. In 1973 production of *ferro-silicon* (75 % basis) was 279,500 tons. Production of *crude steel* was 962,500 tons. The export of products from the electro-metallurgical industries represents 30 % of total exports.

Electro-chemical Industries

The largest concern in the electro-chemical field is *Norsk Hydro*. This firm, which is the largest exporter of nitrogen in Europe, has steadily increased its production. The main product is complex fertilizers and nitrate of lime which is used as a fertilizer, but a number of other chemicals are also produced. Production of estimated pure nitrogen in 1973 was 627,000 tons. Norway is one of the biggest producers of silicon carbide with 50,000 tons (1972).

Iron and Metal Industries

The iron and metal industries employ about 30 % of the total number of industrial workers. They include the *transport equipment* industry, the *machine* industry, the *iron and metal*

37

Norway's Exports and Imports 1974 (mill. kroner)

	Exports		Imports	
Food and feeding stuffs...............		3,280		2,952
Fish and fish preparations	2,065			
Herring meal and other fish meal ..	673			
Cereals and cereal preparations			807	
Fruit and vegetables			658	
Sugar and sugar preparations			532	
Coffee, tea, cocoa, spices			524	
Beverages and tobacco		39		281
Crude materials, inedible except fuels ...		3,055		4,039
Hides, skins and fur skins, undressed	248		41	
Wood, lumber and cork	332		580	
Woodpulp	1,318		420	
Textile fibres	136		131	
Ores and metal scrap	693		1,605	
Fuels, lubricants		2,221		5,720
Animal and vegetable oils and fats		562		223
Chemicals		2,836		4,015
Chemical elements and compounds.	955		1,633	
Fertilizers, manufactured	845		111	
Plastic materials, artificial resins	565		1,044	
Misc. manufactures goods.............		11,192		9,245
Paper, paperboard and manuf.	2,306		576	
Textile yarn, fabrics and made-up articles.........................	404		1,553	
Iron and steel	2,599		3,267	
Non-ferrous metals	4,470		1,080	
Machinery, transport equipment (excl. ships) and misc. manuf. articles		5,352		14,999
Machinery, apparatus and appliances	3,398		7,815	
Transport equipment (excl. ships) ..	690		2,987	
Miscellaneous		103		124
Total, excluding ships		28,640		41,598
Ships		6,080		4,958
Total value		34,720		46,556

goods industry and the *electro-technical* industry. The most important branch is the *shipbuilding* industry, which in 1973 delivered about 950,000 gross tons. The shipbuilding industry is also to a great extent engaged in ship repair work. Production at Norwegian shipyards varies greatly and the facilities for building new ships have been substantially expanded.

The shipbuilding industry has over the last years gained new expertise in fields, which among other things, results from the oil exploration activities on the Norwegian continental shelf. This is particularly the case with the contruction of drilling platforms and supply ships.

The extensive development of hydro-electric power in Norway has created a considerable *electro-technical* industry which produces all types of machines and appliances required by power plants and for the transmission of electric energy and all forms for utilization of electricity.

The machine industry has particularly specialized in supplying production equipment for processing the country's own raw materials. There is also a considerable export of such equipment.

The Food Industries

The food and beverage industries form the second largest group within the traditional domestic industries and employ about 15 % of the total number of industrial workers. These industries are producing an ever increasing variety of products.

The Textile Industry

The textile and garment industry supplies a significant part of Norway's consumption of textiles, clothing and footwear. In recent years this industry has successfully exported a number of specialities. The textile and garment industry employs about 8 % of those engaged in manufacturing industries.

Shipping

At the beginning of 1976 the Norwegian merchant fleet (ships above 100 gross tons) totalled 25,7 mill. gross tons, equivalent to approximately 8.0 per cent of the world tonnage. Only Liberia, Japan and United Kingdom with respectively 65.8, 39.7 and 33.2 mill. gross tons had larger active merchant fleets.

Prior to World War II Norway had a merchant fleet of 4.8 mill. gross tons, equivalent to 7 per cent of world tonnage. The fleet took part in all major allied military operations during the war. Due to heavy war losses the fleet in 1945 was reduced to 2,7 mill. gross tons or 4 per cent of world tonnage. The fleet passed the 5 mill. tons mark in 1950, and was doubled in the following 10 years. Norway has today a modern, efficient fleet, most of which consists of new large ships. The ships employed in foreign trade total more than 97 per cent of the Norwegian merchant fleet. Only few of these ships are engaged in carrying cargoes between Norway and her

Distribution of the fleet

Type of ships	No of ships	1000 grt.	Per cent
Tankers	323	14,018	55,7
Bulk/oil and ore/ oil carriers	56	3,777	15,0
Other bulk carriers	215	5,255	20,9
Other dry cargo	443	1,819	7,2
Passenger ships and ferries	29	302	1,2
Total foreign-going fleet	1,066	25,171	100,0
Supply vessels	94	54	0,2

This turbine tanker of 417,000 tdw. is the largest in the Norwegian fleet (1976). It was delivered in December 1975 from Mitsui Shipbuilding & Engineering Co. Ltd., Japan.

trading partners, or call at Norwegian ports. The shipping industry in Norway is relatively of greater importance to the national economy than is the case in almost any other country in the world.

Distribution of the Fleet

At the beginning of 1976 the total Norwegian fleet including the coastal and fishing fleet, consisted of 2,804 ships above 100 gross tons as described below by type, number and tonnage.

The average size of the Norwegian ships (ships above 500 gross tons) was 23,360 gross tons, compared to 10,210 gross tons in the world fleet, and the average age was 6.2 years per gross ton, compared to 9.3 years per gross ton in the world fleet.

Employment of the Fleet

In the middle of 1975 60 per cent of the tanker tonnage and 61 per cent of the dry cargo tonnage were employed under timecharters, consecutive voyages or other contracts of at least 12 months duration. Approximately 4 per cent of the merchant fleet was employed on

scheduled routes and per March 1976 32,2 per cent of the tonnage was laid up for lack of employment.

Towards the end of 1975 28,400 seamen were employed on board the Norwegian merchant fleet in foreign trade.

If the shipbuilding industry, staff in shipping companies, shipbrokers etc. are included, about 100,000 persons or approximately 7 per cent of the economically active population work in the shipping industry of Norway.

Shipping Companies

Norwegian shipping is a private industry, wholly owned and operated by private individuals and companies. The merchant fleet has been built without government support such as subsidies or cargo preference. In most countries the shipping industry is dominated by only a few firms. In Norway the fleet engaged in international trade is managed by about 300 companies, each of which owns or manages from 1 to 50 ships. The large number of shipping companies has played an important role in the growth and vitality of Norway's shipping industry – and industries such as ship construction, maintenance and supplies, marine insurance and maritime law.

As per 1st January 1976 the 19 Norwegian shipping companies mentioned below operated more than 300,000 gross tons each.

Sig. Bergesen d.y. & Co., Stavanger – 19 ships of 2,250,910 gross tons.

Anders Jahre, Sandefjord – 27 ships of 1,581,069 gross tons.

Hilmar Reksten, Bergen – 13 ships of 1,331,568 gross tons.

Wilh. Wilhelmsen, Oslo – 56 ships of 1,187,000 gross tons.

Leif Høegh & Co. A/S, Oslo – 29 ships of 839,248 gross tons.

Fearnley & Eger, Oslo – 23 ships of 1,008,279 gross tons.

Hagb. Waage, Oslo – 9 ships of 949,255 gross tons.

A/S Thor Dahl, Sandefjord – 11 ships of 647,237 gross tons.

Einar Rasmussen Rederi, Kristiansand – 15 ships of 835,278 gross tons.

Mosvold Rederiene, Kristiansand – 14 ships of 643,057 gross tons.

Jørgen P. Jensen, Arendal – 8 ships of 453,025 gross tons.

Ditlev-Simonsen Rederiene, Oslo – 15 ships of 479,524 gross tons.

Knut Knutsen OAS, Haugesund – 16 ships of 537,924 gross tons.

Sig. Herlofson & Co. A/S – 13 ships of 308,268 gross tons.

Ugland Rederiene, Grimstad – 24 ships of 466,874 gross tons.

P. Meyer, Oslo – 10 ships of 319,821 gross tons.

Odd Godager & Co. A/S, Oslo – 7 ships of 322,993 gross tons.

A/S Olsen & Ugelstad, Oslo – 6 ships of 301,750 gross tons.

C. H. Sørensen & Sønner, Arendal – 6 ships of 459,224 gross tons.

Further Development

The Norwegian shipping industry has undergone a heavy structural change during the last years, and the predominant feature of the tonnage on order has been the ever growing tendency towards larger and more specialized ships.

From 1960 to 1975 33,6 mill. gross tons were delivered to Norwegian shipowners from shipping yards abroad and in Norway. The following table shows the distribution of new-buildings for Norwegian account in 1960–1975.

Building country	1000 gross tons
Sweden	8,659
Japan	9,202
Norway	7,179
West-Germany	3,517
Great-Britain.............	1,388
Other countries	3,673
Deliveries 1960–1975	33,618

The modernization of the Norwegian fleet will continue. As per 1st January 1976, Norwegian shipowners had 7,8 million gross tons of new tonnage on orders equivalent to 9,5 per cent of the total order book in the world. These ships will be delivered up to 1979. The main part of the order reserve consists of large tankers and bulk carriers. Few liner ships have been ordered during the last years and there is no indication that the replacement requirement for the liner fleet will be met during the years to come.

The fleets of Norwegian shipping companies generally consist of modern ships, older vessels being sold to other countries before becoming obsolete. Of the 1–2 mill. grt. annually sold to other countries, most of the ships will continue to be in operation for many years to come.

The development of Norwegian shipping is a result of the natural division of labour between the various countries. The trade is built upon the principle of free competition and the Norwegian merchant fleet is able to offer cheap transport facilities without any form of state subsidies or cargo preference.

Training

The majority of Norwegian seamen come from the coastal districts. Roughly 50 % receive no special training before going to sea. Primary training for young seamen is given at schools or aboard training ships, one of which is a sailing ship. Advanced training is provided by the official seamen's schools in a number of districts. These schools issue certificates for ship's officers, radio officers and other specially trained personnel.

Welfare

Extensive welfare work for sailors is carried out on board and in foreign ports by private institutions, and a government-subsidized welfare organization. The work of the *Norwegian Seamen's Mission* is financed mainly through voluntary contributions from shipowners, Norwegians abroad, associations and the seamen themselves. In the last years the Government has taken active part in the financing of the Norwegian Seamen's Mission and now contributes with 75per cent of the salaries of the seamen's chaplains. Founded in 1864, this organization operates stations in foreign ports with churches, reading rooms etc. and initiates arrangements of social and religious nature.

The State Welfare Council for the Merchant Fleet was organized after World War II and is financed through contributions from the Government, seamen, shipowners and 30 per cent of taxes paid by foreign seamen on Norwegian ships. The Council's branch offices in important ports hold courses, distribute books and films etc., encourage athletics among seamen through instruction and competitions, and also operate clubs for seamen.

Sea Rescue

The work of the *Norwegian Society for Sea Rescue* is financed through voluntary contributions and government support. At present this institution operates 38 motor rescue vessels, all with modern equipment. In the years of operation valuable assistance has been given to fishing vessels and other crafts. The society's rescue ships also provide transport for the sick and give other assistance in emergencies.

Foreign Trade

Due to the economic structure of Norway, the relatively high standard of living can only be maintained through a substantial foreign trade: In 1973 Norway's total imports and exports amounted to U.S. $ 2228 per inhabitant. That year only seven other countries in the world had a greater foreign trade per capita.

Norway's three main trade partners in 1974 were Sweden, W. Germany and the U.K. There is also a lively trade with the U.S.A., Denmark, Finland and the Netherlands as well as France, Italy, Belgium, and large imports from Japan (ships) and Canada (ores). Trade (exports and imports) with the above mentioned countries represents nearly 80 % of Norway's foreign trade.

Exports

Norway's traditional export commodities are *fish, forest products* and some *ores*. Due to the development of hydroelectric power in the 20th century *electro-chemical* and *electro-metallurgical products* have become important export commodities.

In recent years an increasing role has been played by machinery and apparatus and a variety of finished products.

Fish, wood pulp, paper and paperboard are sold all over the world. The electro-metallurgical products (ferro alloys, steel products, aluminium, nickel, zinc, magnesium) mainly go to the U.K., West Germany, Sweden and the U.S.A.; electro-chemical products, mainly nitrogen fertilizer, mostly to the other Scandinavian countries and the U.S.A., but also to other continents. The machine industry exports to all industrial countries in Western Europe, and to U.S.A. and Canada.

Foreign Trade 1974 (ships incl.)

By country	Exports Mill. kr.	%	Imports Mill. kr.	%
Sweden ...	6,085	17,5	8,760	18,8
Finland ...	1,042	3,0	992	2,1
Switzerland	374	1,1	779	1,7
Austria ...	252	0,7	505	1,1
Portugal ..	346	1,0	264	0,6
Iceland ...	243	0,7	81	0,2
EFTA TOTAL	8,342	24,0	11,381	24,4
W. Germany ..	3,629	10,5	6,698	14,4
Denmark..	2,822	8,1	2,631	5,7
United Kingdom	5,768	16,6	4,678	10,0
Belgium-Luxemb.	673	1,9	1,311	2,8
France ...	1,164	3,4	1,445	3,1
Italy	850	2,4	721	1,5
Netherlands	1,301	3,7	1,955	4,2
EEC TOTAL	16,207	46,6	19,439	41,8
USSR	220	0,6	384	0,8
Spain	435	1,3	411	0,9
Czechoslovakia ...	98	0,3	178	0,4
E. Germany	328	0,9	213	0,5
Poland ...	295	0,8	290	0,6
Other European countries	1,040	3,0	412	0,9
EUROPE TOTAL	26,965	77,6	32,708	70,3
Japan	358	1,0	2,902	6,2
ASIA TOTAL	2,172	6,3	5,938	12,8
AFRICA TOTAL	1,959	5,6	1,104	2,4
Canada ...	276	0,8	1,316	2,8
USA	1,847	5,3	3,787	8,1
N.AMERICA TOTAL	2,780	8,0	5,728	12,3
SOUTH AMERICA ..	576	1,7	847	1,8
AUSTRALIA (INCL. OCEANIA) ...	268	0,8	231	0,5
TOTAL ..	34,720		46,556	

In the last years ships have been the most important single item among the export commodities.

Exports of crude mineral oil from the Norwegian part of the Continental shelf in the North Sea started on a small scale in 1971 and is expected to increase considerably in the coming years.

Imports

The main imports are *machines, ships* and other *transport equipment, fuel, metals, food* and *clothing* and *fabrics.* A substantial quantity of metals and ores are processed and re-exported. The substantial imports of ships illustrate the importance of shipping of the country's economy.

Mineral oils and mineral oil products mainly come from the European countries and from the Middle East. Ores and chemicals, which are processed by the electro-metallurgical industry, are mainly aluminium oxide from Jamaica and Guinea, chromium and manganese ores from African countries, and nickel from Canada. Western European countries and Japan build a large number of ships for Norway, while Europe and the U.S.A. are the main sources of supply for machines. The predominant share of motor vehicles is imported from Europe and Japan. Textiles and clothing to supplement domestic production are mainly imported from Europe and developing countries, while Canada and the U.S.A. are the main suppliers of bread grain.

Balance of Payments

Commodity imports exceed exports, the deficit being partly or fully balanced by net earnings of the shipping industry. During most post-war years there have been deficits on current account, because of considerable imports of capital goods due to investments in development of the country's trade and industry. The deficits have been met through public and private imports of capital. Of great significance are foreign loans for the construction of ship for Norwegian shipping companies.

Balance of Payments 1975

A. CURRENT ACCOUNT

Income	Mill. kr.	Expenditure	Mill. kr.
Exports excl. ships	32,296	Imports excl. ships	47,499
Exports of new ships	2,515	Imports of ships	6,583
Exports of second-hand ships	2,946	Ships'exp.abroad	7,905
Freight earnings	16,590	Other services	9,920
Other services etc.	7,050	Interest & transfers	5,052
Interest & transfers	2,292		
Total	63,689	Total	76,959

B. CAPITAL ACCOUNT

Income	Mill. kr.	Expenditure	Mill. kr.
Receipt of long term capital transactions	26,422	Net current account	13,270
		Payments on long-term capital transactions........	12,892
Total	26,422	Total	26,162
Basic balance	− 260	Short-term capital transactions (net)	260

Specification: Increases in foreign exchange reserves: 1370 mill. kr.
Total net gold and foreign exchange
reserves 31. 12. 1975   11,647 mill. kr

Communications

Scattered settlements, the country's great north-south length with deep valleys, high mountains and great fjords, as well as the climatic conditions, are factors which greatly add to the difficulties and cost of maintaining both land communications and telecommunications in Norway.

International Communications

Norway has regular communications by sea with a number of the major cities of many countries. Railroad connections with the Continent run via Sweden and Denmark. The roads are linked with those of the other countries on the Scandinavian Peninsula, and large car ferries maintain regular connections with Denmark, U.K. and Germany. International flights are mainly scheduled via Copenhagen.

Roads

At the end of 1975 Norway had 77,100 kilometres of public roads, 55,600 kilometres of which are maintained by the government and the counties, while the municipalities are responsible for the remainder. In addition to this there is a well developed network of private forest roads for transport of timber. 34,600 kilometres of the public roads (44,8 %) are hardsurfaced, usually bituminous, while the remainder is gravel-surfaced. It is estimated that additional 30,000 kilometres of roads, including a motorway system, are required, and that comprehensive reconstruction of older roads and bridges as well as permanent surfacing is essential.

Part of a new motorway near Oslo.

Motor Vehicles

At the end of 1975 automobiles in Norway totalled 1,100,834 of which 953,657 were passenger cars. This is equivalent to 4,2 inhabitants per passenger car. In addition come 235,830 motor-cycles, agricultural tractors etc. The total number of motor vehicles amounted to 1,336,664.

Buses employed in public transportation at the end of 1973 totalled 9,697, with an annual number of passenger-kilometres (1973) of 3,869 mill. Operation of this service is generally unprofitable but essential to communities lacking other facilities of transportation, and subsidies amounting to 93,1 mill. kroner were appropriated by the government.

The number of automobiles is rapidly increasing, resulting in parking problems in the cities and congested traffic on inadequate roads.

Railways

Norway has 4,241 kilometres of railways (eq. 2,636 miles), 16 kilo-metres owned by private companies, and the rest owned by the Norwegian State Railways. The railways are mainly single tracked and of normal gauge. 58 per cent of the tracks are electrified.

From 1970 electric and diesel engines have replaced the steam engines.

In 1974 the railroads carried 32,6 mill. passengers an average distance of 58 kilometres, and transported 31,3 mill. tons of freight, equivalent to 2,886 mill. ton/kilometres. In 1974 the railways were operated at a total deficit of 354,4 mill. kroner.

Aviation

DNL (Det Norske Luftfartsselskap), Norway's airline, was founded in 1927 by shipping interests. In order to open a route to New York, a venture considered too costly for DNL alone, the Scandinavian Airlines System (SAS) was formed in 1946 in cooperation with the national airlines of Denmark and Sweden. In 1948, the three companies also pooled their European traffic, and

45

Communication along the coast is improved by the building of small airfields. Here is the airfield in Svolvær.

in 1950 they merged all their resources and activities in a new SAS organization. Simultaneously, the Governments of all three countries assumed 50 % of the capital of the respective airlines which now became parent companies of SAS. Norway and Denmark have since then each held 2/7 of the total capital invested in SAS, and Sweden 3/7.

Domestically, a private company, Braathens SAFE Air Transport, now has nearly the same amount of traffic as SAS.

From Bergen, SAS maintains regular non-stop flights to New York and Seattle. Other intercontinental SAS routes originate in Copenhagen, which is served from Oslo 13 times daily. European destinations are either served by direct routes or via Copenhagen.

SAS has concluded agreements with Swissair, KLM and UTA of France for operational and technical cooperation. With THAI Airways, SAS is coowner of THAI International, to which is also given commercial and technical assistance.

In 1974 SAS carried 6,3 million passengers. It is the third largest on European carrier routes and the eighth largest on the North American routes. Widerøes Flyveselskap A/S provides commuter services to 30 communities along the Norwegian coast.

Major Air Fields

The following airfields for international commercial aviation are owned and operated by the government, and are also utilized by a number of foreign air lines with direct flights to Norway:

Bergen (Flesland), Kirkenes (Høybuktmoen), Bodø (Bodø), Kristiansand, (Kjevik), Oslo (Fornebu and Gardermoen), Stavanger (Sola), Tromsø (Langnes), Trondheim (Værnes), Svalbard (Longyear).

Coastal Transport

By extending the road and bridge system and also the ferry connections across the fjords, the need for coastal passenger and freight lines will gradually be reduced, but due to the structure of the country, with deep fjords and many islands, the domestic coastal shipping services will still have an important function.

Approx 440 vessels with a gross tonnage of 106,000 tons are employed in regular coastal service. In addition, 247 vessels totalling

71,000 gross tons run as ferries between public roads, annually carrying 35,9 mill. passengers and 10,8 mill. motor vehicles. This does not include coastal tramp trade.

Postal Service

The postal service was established in 1647 and is operated as a government directorate. The first stamp was issued in 1855. Norway has (Jan. 1974) about 3,201 post offices which annually handle 1,078 mill. mail items, including 667 mill. letter-post. The Post Office (Postverket) also operates a Giro service and a postal Savings Bank.

Telecommunications

In January 1975 there were 1,35 mill. telephones – 33,9 per hundred inhabitants. More than 87,9 % of the telephones are automatically operated, and the number of subscribers connected with the national and international long distance direct dialing system is rapidly being increased. The telephone and telex services are operated by the state Telegraph Service *(Televerket)*.

Mass Media

The Press

Norway's first periodical dates back to 1763, when a small weekly with many advertisements and under the rigid censorship of those days was published in Oslo. The first newspapers in Bergen, Trondheim and Kristiansand appeared in 1765–80. Of these papers, *Adresseavisen* of Trondheim still exists and is the oldest newspaper in Norway. Not until the principle of the freedom of the Press was established in the Constitution in 1814 did the Norwegian Press become an important factor in the formation of public opinion. The first daily *(Morgenbladet)* was issued in 1819. Norway's largest newspaper today, *Aftenposten*, the only paper with two daily editions, was started in 1860.

In recent years the «death rate» of newspapers in Norway has been relatively low compared with other countries. The total number of newspapers declined from 191 in 1950, to 159 in 1973. During the same period total circulation increased by about 23 %, from 1,513,000 in 1950 to 1,870,000 in 1973. Average circulation per newspaper increased from 7,700 to 12,100.

Local newspapers play a very important role in Norwegian press In addition to 8 dailies in the Capital, 72 dailies, some of them of great influence, are published in various parts of the country. Dailies have 6 issues a week, and there are no Sunday editions. In 1975 total newspaper circulation was equivalent to 1,5 newspaper per household.

Of the 80 dailies only three have a net circulation exceeding 100,000

Most of Norways TV-transmitters are erected on tops in the snowy mountains.

copies, (Aftenposten, Conservative, Oslo: morning edition 207,202), VG – Verdens Gang, Independent, Oslo: (146,599), Dagbladet, Liberal, Oslo: (119,429), three 50–100,000 (Bergens Tidende, Liberal, Bergen: 81,050, Adresseavisen, Conservative, Trondheim: 74,681, Arbeiderbladet, Labour, Oslo: 62,211).

Practically all newspapers are politically engaged. However, the political affiliation and the circulation and size of the newspapers seldom correspond. Thus the Labour Party, with 43 % of the votes in the 1969 Storting election, had only 23.7 % of the daily newspaper circulation in 1972.

Technically, the newspapers have made substantial progress since World War II with regard to news service, distribution and methods of production. Even with relatively small newspapers multi-colour printing is quite usual and in January 1973 62 papers had acquired offset facilities.

Press ethics in Norway are on a high level. The Norwegian Press Association (Norsk Presseforbund) has established rules for the protection of the rights of the individual. A professional committee deals with complaints concerning violations of press ethics and makes statements thereon. The independence of the editors is strongly emphasized.

Radio and Television

All Norwegian radio and television transmitters are operated by the Norwegian Broadcasting Corporation (Norsk Rikskringkasting – NRK) which has the monopoly to transmit sound and pictures in Norway. It is an independent, public legal entity. The Director General is responsible to a Board of 5 members, appointed by the King.

Due to the characteristics of the topography and the great distances a relatively large number of transmitters are required to cover the entire country satisfactorily.

At present there are 42 FM transmitters with 265 FM low power rebroadcast stations in operation, 8 long wave transmitters, 29 medium wave and 5 short wave transmitters. In addition there are 43 TV transmitters operating, with a total of 483 low power rebroadcast stations. Future plans include more FM and TV transmitters. The national link distribution circuit has a one-way length of 5036 km, extending as far as Kirkenes. TV coverage has by now reached 95 % of the country. Colour television was introduced January 1st, 1972, to begin with on a three-year introductory basis, aiming at at least 50 % colour programmes by 1975.

The most powerful Norwegian broadcasting station is at Kløfta, near Oslo, with 200 kW, and operating on long wave (218 kHz or 1376 meters). Norwegian programmes are of an informative and educational nature rather than purely entertaining. NRK transmit no commercial advertising or sponsored programmes. News and weather reports at 0600, 0700, 0730, 0800, 1000, 1230, 1400, 1700, 1830, 2200 and 2400 hrs GMT.

Special broadcasts to the merchant fleet and Norwegians abroad are transmitted via the short wave stations at Fredrikstad. The programmes, which are in Norwegian with short announcements in English, are broadcast 12–15 times daily.

Every Sunday there is a programme in English, Norway this Week, and a programme in Spanish, La Semana en Noruega, following the special Norwegian broadcast.

Health

The public health services are administered by the Health Services of Norway, a directorate within the Ministry of Social Affairs. The directorate has divisions which handle matters dealing with general hygiene, epidemics, infectious diseases, mental health and mental diseases, social medicine and nursing and also act as a supervising authority for medical personnel, among others; medical officers dentists, hospitals and pharmacies.

Local administration of health control and sanitation is performed which the local public health officer is chairmen. The members of the local health boards are elected by the municipal councils. There must be at least one woman on each board.

Medical Services

Norway has about 6500 licenced physicians younger than 70 years, or 1 doctor per 615 inh. Most of them are working in hospitals. Specialists are mainly found in the larger towns. There are approx. 1000 midwives and 28,000 registered nurses, while qualified personnel in pharmacies (druggists), number 800.

Due to geographic conditions there are a number of small general hospitals. In most parts of the country, however, there are central hospitals with many specialists and modern equipment for diagnosis and treatment. 80 per cent of hospitals are owned by the State, the counties or municipalities. 20 per cent are semi-private and operated by religious or social organizations such as Norwegian Red Cross, Norwegian Women's Health Organization and the Catholic Church etc.

Thanks to extensive preventive measures and the introduction of new methods of treatment after World War II, the decrease in the occurrence of tuberculosis has been remarkable. Under a law of 1947, X-ray control, tuberculin testing and BCG-vaccination of persons with negative reaction to tuberculin test, can be made compulsory by order of the Ministry of Social Affairs.

Norway's National Mass Radiography Service is now introducing a new system for watching Tb-risk-groups, – a system which aims at more frequent examinations of persons who in regard to tuberculosis of the lung, constitute a greater risk than others. Such risk groups are selected on the basis of statistical material mainly obtained from the National Tuberculosis Register and from results from mass-radiography surveys (lung-lesion tuberculin-reaction, BCG-vaccination, Height/weight ratio etc.).

There is a well-developed system

Principal Causes of Death, per 100,000 population, 1973

ISCHAEMIC HEART DISEASES....	270,2
CANCER......................	187,5
CEREBROVASCULAR DISEASES....	155,5
PNEUMONIA...................	64,9
ACCIDENTS, HOMICIDE, SUICIDE...................	62,0
INDEFINITE CAUSES...........	52,0
TOTAL (all causes).........1008,9	

Møre & Romsdal County Hospital in Ålesund.

of maternal and child health control, while a statute of 1957 makes the provision of school health services compulsory for all state schools.

A new Act put into force 1st April 1974 states that it is the responsibility of each local Authority to establish Child Welfare Clinics to provide all children with health control and necessary preventive measures free of charge. Immunisation programmes are carried through against Smallpox, Diphteria, Pertussis, Tetanus Polio and Measles.

Family Counselling Services, given by professional teams and integrated into the public health services, are free of charge, paid for partly by the Health Insurance, and partly by the state, while possible deficit is paid for by the owner (the county or private organization). This important preventive mental health service is planned in every province.

According to the Mental Health Act of 1961 the counties will have to provide mental health care for the persons requiring such aid. Examination, treatment and care in mental institutions, policlinics, pre-care and after-care, are paid for by the Health Insurance (see page 54), and by the municipality. At present more than 17,000 patients are under treatment and care.

Under the Hospital Act of 1969 the municipalities have the same responsibilities for the mentally retarded. About 8000 are given treatment, training and care in institusions and day centres for mentally retarded. The campaign against drug abuse is led by «Sentralrådet for narkotikaproblemer» (National Narcotics advisory Board).

As of 31st December 1974, a public system of home nursing had been introduced in 348 out of the country's 444 local municipalities. Personnel employed in this activity at the same time totalled 1314 authorized nurses and 598 practical nurses with publicly recognized training.

Dental Care

There were 3,800 dentists in Norway in 1973, or one per 1,150 inhabitants. One third of the dentists work in the school dental service or the public dental service as salaried personnel. Systematic, dental care is provided free of charge for children 6–17 years of age. In some municipalities even preschool children are included among the patients of the public service.

Generally, dental services for the adult population are provided by private practitioners and paid for on a fee-for-service basis out of the pockets of the patients.

No water fluoridation project is in operation. The use of fluoride tablets is recommended and topical application of fluoride takes place on a large scale in public programmes for children.

Health Organizations

The most important voluntary health organizations are: *Norsk Folkehjelp* (Norwegian People's Relief Association) – 700,000 members. *Norges Røde Kors* (Norwegian Red Cross) – 322,200 members. *Norske Kvinners Sanitetsforening* (Norwegian Women's Public Health Association – 250,000 members. *Nasjonalforeningen for Folkehelsen* (National Public Health Association) – 200,000 members. *Landsforeningen mot kreft* (Norwegian Cancer Society) – 145,000 members.

Social Conditions

The National Insurance

On 1st January 1967 the social insurance system underwent far-reaching changes. The National Insurance Act *(Folketrygden)* then came into force. The social insurances in Norway had previously aimed mainly at ensuring a minimum standard for everybody. Folketrygden, "people's security", is an expression of the view that the entire population should be ensured a standard of living reasonably relative to the standard built up by the individual during his working life, also in old age, disability and loss of supporter.

The National Insurance Scheme is compulsory for all who are residents in Norway. It replaced several of the benefits previously in existence and increased the benefits. In the first phase it included *Old Age Benefit, Disability Benefit* and *Rehabilitation Assistance, Widows' and Mothers' Benefit* and *Survivors' Benefit for Children.* From 1st January 1971 Medical Care and Sickness Benefits *(Health Insurance), Occupational Injury Insurance* and *Unemployment Insurance* were included. The *Family Allowance Scheme,* which is financed in full by the State, is not an insurance in the literal sense and not included in the National Insurance Scheme. The same applies to the *War Pensions* which are of limited duration and of a special nature.

What is new in the National Insurance Scheme, making it a considerably better arrangement than the previous insurance schemes, is first and foremost the *Supplementary Pensions* which are graded according to income. Most pensions will consist of two parts: A *Basic Pension* which is independent of the income, and a *Supplementary Pension* which varies according to income and pension-earning time. According to the Act on National Insurance the benefits shall be stipulated in relation to a basic amount. The basic amount is to be adjusted each year in accordance with the changes in the general income level and the cost of living. As from 1st May 1975 the basic pension has been fixed at Nkr. 11 000 a year for single persons and Nkr. 16.500 for couples.

Old Age Pension

On 1st January 1973 the pensionable age was lowered from 70 years to 67 years.

The basic pension is as a main rule paid in full from 1967. The supplementary pension must normally be worked up through a period of 40 years. In a transition period special rules apply, so that all persons who were younger than 50 years when the Act came into force, can work up a full supplementary pension. For those who are over 50 years each pension-earning year counts double. These special rules apply only to that part of the income that does not exceed five times the basic amount. Only persons born in 1898

51

The Norwegian National Insurance Scheme.

Pensions and transitional benefits by type of benefit. 1975.

Benefit	In December 1975		Costs 1975[2])
	Number of recipients	Yearly amount per recipient[1])	
		Kroner	Million kroner
Old age pension	464,164	13,780	5,873,6
Disability pension	142,542	17,375	2,695,9
Survivor's pension/transitional benefits (surviving spouse, unmarried person forced to live at home)	45,244	14,705	667,1
Children's pension	25,309	4,004	105,6
Transitional benefits to unmarried mothers	12,369	12,236	149,3
Total	689,655	14,197	9,491,5

[1]) Including special supplement and compensation supplement.
[2]) Including special supplement, compensation supplement, basic grant and assistance grant for disabled, assistance benefit for surviving spouse and unmarried mother.

or later qualify for the supplementary pension.

Full Supplementary Pension is equal to 45 % of pensionable income in excess of the basic amount. However, as regards income between 8 and 12 times the basic amount, account is only taken of $\frac{1}{3}$ of such income, and no account is taken of income exceeding 12 times the basic amount.

Full Basic Pension for a single person is equal to the basic amount. A married couple, both of whom are entitled to old age pension, receive 150 % of the basic amount. A compensation supplement (Nkr. 500 for a single person and Nkr. 750 for couples) comes in addition to the basic pension. A special supplement equal to 18 % of basis amount for a single person and 16,75 % of basic amount when the spouse is entitled to a pension, is given to persons who do not have right to supplementary pension. An old age pensioner is entitled to a dependency supplement if he supports a wife and/or children under 18 years.

The *supplementary benefit in respect of a spouse* is equal to 50 % of the basic pension. The *supplement for each dependent child* is equal to 25 % of the basic amount.

The care of old people is primarily the concern of the local authorities. Apart from the services provided by the local authorities, a great deal is done by private organisations, usually with financial support from the local authority and from the government. The government department responsible for the care of old people is Sosialdepartement (The Ministry of Social Affairs), where a special «Old People's Office» was set up in 1971.

«Rådet for eldreomsorgen» (The Council for Old People's welfare) is a body appointed by the government, its members being representatives of private organisations, of local government authorities, and of the central government. The Council is intended to work as a central advisory and coordinating body for the social welfare of old people.

There are at present about 850 Old People's Homes and Geriatric Nursing Homes in the country. Also 50–60 Health and Welfare Centres have been set up. It is the job of centres of this type to assist old people living at home with different and various kinds of services to the best of their ability. Nearly all local authorities employ home-helps for old people. 265 authorities have established a home-nursing service for old people. The home-help service is paid for by the local authorities, 35 per cent being refunded by the government; the government also refund 75 per cent of the cost of the home-nursing service. Old people can also avail themselves of low-interest government loans for structural improvements to their homes.

Assistance supplementary to one's own efforts

The National Insurance Scheme grants several benefits to help the disabled and certain other groups to support themselves fully or partly. Assistance is also given towards rehabilitation and training.

The Rehabilitation Assistance may be granted in the form of rehabilitation allowance, basic grant and assistance grant to persons who, on account of illness, injury or defect, have a permanently reduced capacity for work, or who are handicapped in the choice of occupation. A surviving spouse may also be granted various forms of benefit in order to become self-dependent from his-her own work. The same applies to housebound unmarried persons who have taken care of parents or other near relatives. It applies also to unmarried mothers and divorced persons who have not remarried after the death of their previous spouse.

Disability Benefits

In order to qualify for a disability pension the insured person must be above the age of 18, and the disability must be due to illness, injury or defect which has led to perma-

nent reduction of at least 50 % in capacity for work. Before a disability pension is paid rehabilitation must have been tried unless the insured person is 64 years or older. Full disability pensions will on certain conditions constitute the same amount as the old age pension that the person would have received if he had continued to work till he would have reached pensionable age. It is a precondition that the pension shall be graded according to the remaining capacity for work.

A supplementary benefit is granted for a spouse and dependent children. A disabled person may also be granted other forms of benefit from the National Insurance Scheme.

Survivor's Benefits

When a married person dies, the widow or the widower may on the same conditions be granted the normal basic pension plus 55 % of the supplementary pension that the deceased person would have received on reaching pensionable age. The pension is reduced according to certain rules when the surviving spouse has his/her own income from work.

Children under the age of 18 who lose one of their parents are entitled to a pension. The eldest child will (1975) receive Nkr. 4,400, and each of the other children will receive Nkr. 2,750. If both parents die, the eldest child receives a pension equal to the full pension for a surviving spouse, the next eldest receives Nkr. 4,400 and so on.

Lump Sum Death Benefit

In respect of every death, whether it involves a child or an adult, the National Insurance Scheme provides burial aid with a lump sum payment equal to 20 % of the basic amount. In addition a lump sum benefit equal to 25 % of the basic amount is provided if the deceased is survived by a spouse, or had the custody of children.

Medical Care and Sickness Benefits. (Health Insurance)

The National Insurance Scheme secures free medical care in health institutions, compensations for doctors' fees and free medicines for certain chronic illnesses. A number of other benefits in kind are also provided according to the stipulation of the Act. Furthermore, both wage earners and selfemployed persons are included in a system securing cash benefits during illness or pregnancy.

Occupational Injuries Insurance

All wage earners, students and trainees are insured against occupational injuries and diseases. This scheme may be extended to include self-employed persons (optional).

An injured person is entitled to free medical treatment and possibly to financial support should his earning capacity be permanently reduced or lost. This insurance also covers pensions for widows and dependents.

Unemployment Insurance

All wage-earners are insured against unemployment. Subject to certain conditions, the insured person is in the event of enforced unemployment entitled to a cash allowance, which may vary with other sources of income. For wage-earners over 64 years, as well as independent tradesmen over 64 years, special and more favourable rules have been established. Benefits during unemployment also comprise financial assistance for vocational training and towards finding new means of livelihood. Grants are also provided for moving to another locality, where the beneficiary has been secured a new job.

Administration

The National Insurance Institution is, except for the benefits granted during unemployment, the central authority with county boards, insurance secretariats and insurance offices as the local bodies. The income tax authorities compute the pensionable income and the contribution, and see to it that the contribution is collected.

The unemployment benefits are centrally administered by the Labour Directorate and locally by the county employment offices and the district employment offices.

An Appeal Board has been set up for matters relating to insurance.

Financing the National Insurance Scheme

The costs of the National Insurance Scheme are met by way of contributions from members and employers and payments from the State and the municipalities. As from 1st January 1975 the contribution for members is fixed at 4.5 % of the pensionable income. The employer's contribution is fixed at 17.0 % for 1975. In certain regions of the country the employer's contribution is fixed at a reduced rate, minimum 14 %. For selfemployed persons the premium is 13.0 % of the pensionable income in 1975. Public payments by the State and the municipalities are fixed at 4,5 % of pensionable income and are distributed with one half on each. In addition to this, the members will during 1975 pay 4.4 % of their assessed income. This replaces the former premium for health insurance.

Contributions from employees are not taxfree except part of the contribution from selfemployed person which exceeds the contribution from employees. On the other hand employers' contributions are deductable. The pensions are taxable income. Old age pensioners are from 1970 entitled to a tax reduction. The disabled is likewise from 1971 entitled to the same tax reduction or one half of this reduction in accordance with the degree of lost working capacity.

Family Allowances

From 1970 the Family Allowances' Act was amended so that the benefit is paid for all children under 16 years of age. In the cases where one parent alone maintains the child or children, benefits are now paid for the actual number of children plus one in addition.

Social Care

The Public Assistance Act of 1900 was for many years the only form of public support to persons who were unable to support themselves, and who were not eligible for benefits from insurances or other social benefits.

In 1964 the Public Assistance Act was replaced by a new *Act on Social Care*, which provides that every municipality shall have a publicly elected body, *Social Welfare Board*, wich shall co-ordinate the social work in the municipality. This board shall have at least 5 members. Furthermore, there shall usually be a special *Child Welfare Committee* and a *Temperance Committee*. The assistance that is provided under the new Act aims first and foremost at making the applicant self-supporting and independent of social aid in the future. Therefore the advisory and guidance service constitutes an important part of the responsibility that rests with the Social Welfare Board. Assistance to provide the necessities of life shall be given when it is impossible to make the applicant financially self-supporting. The Social Welfare Board may also, subject to certain conditions, grant the aid in the form of loans or guarantees for loans.

A social welfare office is to be set up in every municipality in accordance with the Act. The office shall deal with the administrative side of the Social Welfare Board's activity.

Child Welfare

Public child welfare is governed by the Child Welfare Act of 1953. This Act provides that there shall be a Child Welfare Committee in every municipality. It shall have 5 members – women and men – with special insight into and interest in child welfare. In special cases, the municipal councils, with the consent of the Ministry of Social Affairs, may decide that the municipality shall not nominate its own Child Welfare Committee. In this event the Social Welfare Board acts as Child Welfare Committee and in accordance with the rules of the Child Welfare Act. The Child Welfare Committees shall carry on general preventive work, take special protective measures to assist certain children, under the age of 18, who stand in need of help, have the supervision of foster children and child welfare institutions and shall conduct an efficient after-care protection.

After the Act on Social Care (see above) was passed in 1964, the Social Welfare Board has had the right to decide that a case being dealt with by the Child Welfare committee shall be handled by the Social Welfare Board if it concerns a family with various types of social problems. The object is that a family shall be given help by the Social Welfare Board to solve all problems. Coercive measures within child welfare can, however, only be decided by the Child Welfare Commitee on the basis of proposals from the Social Welfare Board. In these cases the Town or District Judge shall sit as a member of the Child Welfare Committee.

The County Governor supervises the child welfare work in the county, and all counties in Norway have their own child welfare secretary.

Children's Homes

There are 140 children's homes (including creches and homes for young people in care) accommodating about 1,800 children/young people.

Most of these are small with from 8–12 children/young people. It is not permitted to build new homes for more than 12 children. The institutions and their leaders are approved by the Ministry of Social Affairs. Both the Ministry and the County Governor have a responsibility for supervision of these institutions through the local Child Welfare Committee.

Protection of Mother and Child

A woman is entitled to certain benefits in the event of childbirth. The National Insurance pays confinement expenses and also a "maternity allowance". Legislation provides for financial assistance to mothers in difficult circumstances prior to, and for a certain period after confinement. (See under the National Insurance Scheme.)

Legislation also provides for maintenance allowances to be paid by the father of a child in case of divorce or separation or in case of illegitimacy, and makes provisions for collecting such allowances through public offices, and for advance payment of these allowances. There are also provisions for family allowances. See under the National Insurance Scheme on benefits to survivors.

On 1st January 1972, a provisional Act came into force, under which divorced or separated persons with dependents are entitled to «family allowances» from the public authorities, if they are in financial difficulties.

Labour Protection

Worker's Protection Act of 7th December 1956 applies to every establishment – with certain exceptions – which employs workers or which uses mechanical power of one horsepower or more, (employee – any person who performs work outside his own home in the service of another).

The Act contains provisions concerning measures for ensuring healthy and safe working conditions, hours of work, night work, work on Sundays and public holidays, etc., overtime, special provisions respecting the employment of women (protection of mothers), children and young persons, the payment of wages, dismissal, employment rules etc. and also concerning Labour Inspection. The Workers' Protection Act has with certain amendments of 1973 been applied to Svalbard (Spitsbergen). The act is at present being revised.

Legislation on the Participation of Employees in Decision-making

In 1972 new legislation regarding industrial democracy was adopted. Regulations have thus been established for extending employee participation in the decisionmaking process in the joint-stock companies of a certain size.

Holidays with Pay

The Holiday Act of 1947 instituted a minimum holiday of 18 days a year with full pay. An amendment of 1964 gave all employees 4 weeks' holiday.

Employment Policy and Regional Development

Norway has a comprehensive system of labour exchange offices with the Labour Directorate as the central institution. In recent years central and local authorities for regional planning and district development has been built out and strengthened. The Ministry of Local Government and Labour is the central coordinating authority.

The Government leads an active labour market policy to promote full and productive employment. Special efforts are made to secure a balanced development between the various geographical regions and districts. As a consequence of greater emphasis on welfare and social aspects, the problems of special groups have come more into the foreground as well.

An important policy instrument is to stimulate the establishment of new industries in the poorly developed districts by offering certain grants and benefits. Another measure is the promotion of geographical and vocational mobility of the labour force, especially by vocational training for adults. The rapid structural change in economic life makes this a very urgent concern.

Priority is also given to the rehabilitation of the handicapped and measures aimed at tackling the problems of older workers.

Trade Unions

The first Norwegian trade unions for workers in manufacturing industries were formed around 1870. Around 1900 workers in the building trades also became organized. Today there are 40 national trade unions, comprising workers in manufacturing and building industries as well as in agriculture and fisheries, and also employees in private enterprises and government offices.

These unions constitute the *Federation of Trade Unions* (LO) which was founded in 1899 and today (1976) has about 650,000 members.

Within the Federation, the *Norwegian Confederation of Salaried Employees* has been established to co-ordinate the activities of all unions for non-manual workers. These unions, which number 19, have about 170,000 members.

Employers' Association

The employers are correspondingly organized, their central organization being the *Norwegian Employers' Confederation* (NAF). This organization mainly represents enterprises engaged in manufacturing and inland transportation. Member firms number about 8,400 employing about 365,500 workers (1/1 1975).

Labour Conflicts

Disputes arising from collective agreements are decided by the Labour Court whose decisions are inappellable. Disputes where collective agreements do not exist are generally settled through negotiations between a trade union and the employer, sometimes between the two central organizations. In such disputes strikes and lockouts are considered legal. But a system of arbitration exists which is administered by the office of the National Arbitrator.

Education

In Norway all children are entitled to education, and school attendance is also compulsory. Education is mainly provided by public schools, but there are also private educational institutions, the professional standard of which must be approved by the Ministry of Church and Education.

Public schools are run by the municipality, the county and the State, and no fees are paid. Most

private schools receive some financial support from the municipality and the state.

Primary Schools

The Royal Ordinance of 1739 was the origin of compulsory primary school education.

During the first hundred years the

curriculum comprised only reading and religion, later arithmetic and writing were included. During the last half of the 19th century geography, history and some handicrafts were added to the curriculum.

In rural districts with a sparse population there are still some schools with only one teacher, and where children of different grades are being taught in the same classroom. In more densely populated areas and in the towns there is always at least one classroom for each grade.

A 7 year compulsory primary school system was introduced at the end of the 19th century, but acknowledging the necessity of further education for all in a modern society, a Primary School Act was adopted in 1959, authorizing the municipalities to extend the period of compulsory school attendance from seven to nine years.

The 9 Year Primary School

This school is organized as a six-year lower stage school *(barneskole)* plus a three-year upper stage school *(ungdomsskole)* with an optional tenth grade. The number of optional subjects in the curriculum for the eighth and ninth grades has been increased. The nine year school has been run on an experimental basis since 1954. An act concerning its general introduction was passed by Parliament (Stortinget) in 1969. The 9 years basic school now forms the basis for all secondary education, replacing the former continuation school (framhaldskole) and a lower secondary school (realskole).

Secondary Schools

There are a number of different types of schools on the upper secondary level (10th–12th school year) which are based on the completed nine-year primary school: the secondary school, upper stage *(gymnas)* and the commercial secondary school *(øko-nomisk gymnas)*, vocational schools for handicraft and industry, vocational schools for commerce, vocational schools for domestic science, maritime schools and fishery schools.

Some of these secondary schools have a very long history. Norway's oldest gymnas, the cathedral schools, thus date back to the middle of the 12th century. Today, the gymnas provides a general education with the curriculum organized in various lines (the English Line, Natural Science Line, Science Line, Latin Line, etc.). This leads to the so-called «examen artium» (leaving certificate) which until now has been the best guarantee for admission to the country's universities and higher institutions of learning.

Today, there are about 60,000 students attending the 180 different gymnas in Norway.

The various vocational schools have generally emerged in the 20th century to meet the increasing needs for trained personnel in industries and trades, and since the World War II these schools have been expanded considerably. Today, the vocational schools for handicraft and industry alone cover the educational requirements for close to 70 trades.

The vocational schools show a considerable variation in structure with courses varying in length from six months to three years. They combine theoretical instruction with practical training in school workshops, in agriculture, forestry, etc. The one-year course is the most common. In addition to the vocational training available through the school system, Norway has a well-developed apprenticeship system in the handicraft and industrial trades, with practical training in companies usually lasting for four years.

There are about 75,000 pupils currently attending vocational schools in Norway and about 50 per cent of all 17 year-olds attend some type of vocational school. The following list shows the main types of schools and the number of schools and pupils (1972):

	Schools	Pupils
Schools for agriculture	60	3 012
Schools for handicraft and industry	186	31 215
Schools for transport and communication	52	5 546
Schools for administration and economy	123	16 145
Schools for health and social services	84	6 579
Other vocational schools	93	4 370

The present school system comprising a number of separate schools on the secondary level is in the process of being revised. In 1974 the Storting passed the «Act concerning upper secondary schools», entailing that a number of vocational schools will be merged with the gymnas to form one school category with various study specialities. The current reform of the school system is based on extensive structural experiments which have been conducted in both the gymnas and the vocational schools for several years. The most important aim of the new act, which entered into force on 1st January 1976, is to create an upper secondary school with an organization and capacity which will in time make it possible to offer everyone the *right* to attend school three years after completing the nine-year primary school and the opportunity to *choose on an unrestricted basis* the field of study.

Special Schools

Educational facilities are also provided for handicapped children. A majority of these facilities are boarding schools, but in urban areas there are a number of day schools. Education is provided for the blind, the deaf, the retarded, children with speech difficulties, and for maladjusted children and youth.

Folk High Schools

are boarding schools providing general education for youth over 17 years of age, almost evenly recruited from rural and urban districts. They offer one – and two – year courses comprising some compulsory subjects but with the main emphasis on voluntary subjects to be selected by the schools themselves. The Folk High Schools, of which in 1974/75 there were 85 with approximately

Children attending an elementary school.

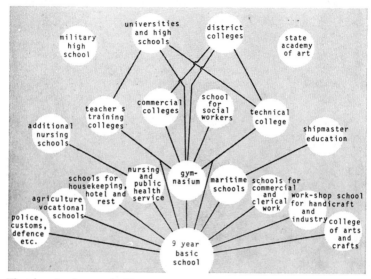

The educational system in Norway.

7600 students, are in general free from examination requirements.

Education of Teachers

Primary school teachers are trained at teachers training colleges, with a two year course for those who have completed secondary school and a four year course for those who have completed primary school, upper stage. Most of the 17 state-run teacher colleges, which in 1971/72 were attended by 7939 students, also offer an extra year of training in special subjects. Two such one-year courses in addition to the basic training, qualify for teaching in the top three classes of the basic school.

A new Law entered into force the autumn of 1975, making provisions for an extension of the normal two years training course to three years. According to this law, the training institutions will be termed pedagogical colleges.

Most secondary school teachers hold university degrees, candidatus magisterii, candidatus realium or candidatus philologiae. The first degree

usually requires about 5 years of study at the university, while the latter two require 6 and 7 years respectively.

There are also higher facilities of learning for teachers of gymnastics, domestic science, arts etc.

Universities and Equivalent Institutions

In 1975 40,000 students attended the universities and about 3 000 Norwegians studied abroad. 15,000 (1975) students attended post-secondary institutions outside the universities and teacher training colleges. During recent years the number of students has greatly increased and is by 1985 expected to reach 80,000 (incl. approx. 15 % students in posteducation).

There are universities in Oslo. Bergen and Trondheim, and a fourth university was established in Tromsø in 1968. So far, teaching in Tromsø takes place in science, the humanities and medicine. Four district colleges were started in 1969. Another two started in 1971. The studies are on bachelor level (2–3 years post-secondary education).

The University of Oslo was founded in 1811. It has seven faculties: theology (there is also an independent Theological college beside that of the University), law, medicine, humanities, natural sciences, social sciences, and odontology.

Number of students (1972): 18 868. Degrees require from 4 to 8 years study.

To some extent student attendance at lectures is mandatory, but the time a student may take before entering for an examination is optional. The university year has generally two terms, autumn and spring, although in some instances there is also a summer term.

An International Summer School, which is attached to the University, was in 1972 attended by 240 students from 29 countries. All lectures are in English.

The University of Bergen, founded in 1948, has the following faculties: law, medicine, humanities, natural sciences, social sciences and odontology. Students numbered 7239 (72). The syllabus and degree requirements are the same as those of the University of Oslo.

The Norwegian Institute of Technology (Norges tekniske høgskole) in Trondheim was founded in 1910, and was in 1972 attended by 1785 students. Degrees in mining, construction, electrical engineering, chemistry, mechanical engineering and applied physics generally require 4–5 years of study. Architects are trained here as well as at the State College of Architecture in Oslo.

The Norwegian Institute of Technology and the State College for Teachers are from 1968 parts of the University of Trondheim.

The Agricultural College of Norway (Norges Landbrukshøgskole) at Ås near Oslo, founded 1897, engages in research and trains specialists in agriculture, horticulture, forestry, dairying and land re-allocation. In 1972, 600 students.

The Veterinary College of Norway (Norges Veterinærhøgskole) in Oslo, founded 1935. Degrees require generally 6 years of study. In 1972, 220 students.

The Norwegian College of Economics and Business Administration (Norges Handelshøyskole) in Bergen, founded 1936. Degrees in business and social economics, jurisprudence and administration generally require 3 years of study, while a teacher's degree requires 4 years. In 1972, 889 students.

The State College for Teachers (Norges Lærerhøgskole) at Lade near Trondheim was founded 1922. Provides supplementary training for primary school teachers for obtaining a university degree. In 1972, 2061 students. University degrees can be taken in humanities, social sciences and natural sciences.

The State College for Sport (Norges Idrettshøgskole) in Oslo, founded 1968, is planned for about 300 students. Two years training qualifies for positions as gymnastics instructors and consultants, and athletics instructors in the armed forces etc.

The State College of Fisheries, (Norges fiskerihøgskole) founded in 1971, provides advanced education and carries out research in fishing. At present teaching takes place at the Norwegian College of Economics and Business Administration and at the universities in Bergen, Trondheim and Tromsø. The intention is that the University of Tromsø, as it expands, shall take over more of both teaching and research.

The State Academy of Art, (Statens kunstakademi) in Oslo, founded in 1909, trains black-and-white artists, painters and sculptors. Courses normally last for three years.

The State College of Music (Musikkhøgskolen) in Oslo was founded in 1972.

Student Loans

The Government Loan Fund for Education (Statens lånekasse for *utdanning)* provides loans for financing studies at universities and colleges, and for pracitically all professional and vocational training of at least one year's duration. The latter requirement may in some cases be waived. The Fund also allocates government scholarships. No interest is paid on the loans during the period of study, and loans are normally repaid by instalments over a period up to 15 years.

Science and Research

Scientific and research activities in Norway were formerly closely linked with the culture and natural resources of the country.

Notable results have been achieved in *archeology* and related studies. Excavations of the Oseberg and Gokstad viking ships, with their rich finds, restorations of the unique stave churches and studies of rune inscriptions and Old Norse sagas, have contributed greatly towards an understanding of the way of life and the beliefs and thoughts of ancient Norwegians and their relations with other European cultures.

In the exploration of Arctic and Antarctic regions Norwegians have played an important part. Names like *Fridtjof Nansen, Roald Amundsen* and *Otto Sverdrup* are forever linked with famous polar discoveries and feats of daring and bravery from pole to pole.

For generations the ocean has been an important source of income for the country through fishing, sealing and whaling. It is therefore natural that Norwegian scientists would interest themselves in *oceanography, marine biology* and *meteorology.* Men like *Michael* and *Ossian Sars, Johan Hjort* and *Bjørn Helland-Hansen* have contributed greatly to the knowledge of ocean currents and the annual migrations of fish, and *Vilhelm Bjerknes* was one of the creators of modern meteorology.

Norwegian mathematicians and physicists have been particularly active in research on cosmic rays and the Northern Lights. *Kristian*

Birkeland, Carl Størmer, Lars Vegard and *Svein Rosseland* have made fundamental contributions in these fields.

Birkeland is also known for his development of the method of extraction of nitrogen from the air, which led to the establishment of the Norwegian Hydro-Electric Nitrogen Company *(Norsk Hydro).*

Armauer Hansen is known as the discoverer of the leprosy bacillus, and in later years important contributions have been made in medicine and in vitamin research by Norwegian doctors and scientists.

In 1969 two Norwegian scientists were awarded the Nobel prize, professor *Odd Hassel* in physical chemistry and professor *Ragnar Frisch* in econometrics.

Activities today

Since World War II, science and research have evolved as parts of an overall national science policy. To co-ordinate the efforts in the different fields, three research councils were established: *The Agricultural Research Council of Norway* (NLVF), *The Norwegian Research Council for Science and the Humanities* (NAVF), *The Royal Norwegian Council for Scientific and Industrial Research* (NTNF).

Within their respective fields they are charged with the task of promoting and co-ordinating research activities and ensuring that the results of these efforts are being used for the benefit of the country. They stimulate the recruitment of research personnel through fellowship programmes and they give grants to research activities in the universities and the various research intitutes. All three councils have panels of committees assisting them in evaluating the different research activities thus enabling them to strengthen activities in fields that are considered to have the highest national priorities.

The activities of the Councils also include operation of research stations and institutes.

Culture

Language

The Norwegian language is closely related to the other Scandinavian languages and to a lesser degree to English, Dutch and German. The various parts of the country have widely differing dialects. Until the end of the 19th century there was only one official language (*riksmål*, later called *bokmål*), strongly influenced by the long union with Denmark. About 1850 a new language was created (then *landsmål*, now *nynorsk* = Neo Norwegian) based on the dialects. The two languages now have equal status in official use and in the schools.

There is great disagreement as to whether the two languages should be amalgamated at a relatively early date or whether they should be permitted to develop naturally towards a common language (*samnorsk*). Illiteracy is nonexistent.

The *Lapps* in northern Norway, who number about 20,000, have kept their own language, which is of Finno-Ugrian origin.

Literature

The oldest literary documents in Norway are the *Eddic poems*, which were probably composed in the 9th or 10th century. The Icelandic sagas have had a great influence on Norwegian national sentiment, especially "*Heimskringla*" (The Globe), written by Snorre Sturlasson. This work presents a brilliant account of Norse mythology and early history up to 1177. "*Kongespeilet*" (The King's Mirror) provides a broad picture of life in medieval Norway.

After the Black Death (1349–50) and during the ensuing union with Denmark, Danish became the official language in Norway, and Norwegian contributions to the common literature were few and insignificant. *Petter Dass* (1647–1707) was an exception. His hymns and folk life poetry became immensely popular, especially in North Norway. In the classical era the Norwegian-born *Ludvig Holberg* (1684–1754) gained a prominent position as author of comedies, epistles and mock-heroic poems. Norwegian traditions, however, survived in the country districts in legends and folklore.

After the dissolution of the union with Denmark in 1814, *Henrik Wergeland* (1808–45) became the dominating figure with his visionary romantic poetry, giving him rank as Norway's greatest poet. Some of his nationalistic ideas were championed by *Bjørnstjerne Bjørnson* (1832–1910), poet, writer of dramas and novels. First taking his motifs from Norse history, he gradually developed into a modern realist. The same development is found in the plays of *Henrik Ibsen* (1828–1906), the dramatist of world fame who was, however, more concerned with personal ethical issues. Other important realistic writers were *Jonas Lie* (1833–1908), *Alexander Kielland* (1849–1906) and *Arne Garborg* (1851–1924). In the 1890's *Hans E. Kinck* (1865–1926) and especially *Knut Hamsun* (1859–1952)

The Hardanger fiddle (Hardingfelen) is a national instrument.

created a new lyrical style in Norwegian prose.

The great realistic novelists of this century, *Sigrid Undset* (1882–1949), *Olav Duun* (1876–1939) and *Johan Falkberget* (1879–1967) have been particularly occupied with ethical issues, often against a historical background. A great lyrical evolution was inaugurated around 1910 by *Olaf Bull* (1883–1933), *Herman Wildenvey* (1886–1959), *Arnulf Øverland* (1889–1968) and *Olav Aukrust* (1883–1929). The prose writers of the pre-war generation include *Nordahl Grieg* (1902–1943), *Sigurd Hoel* (1890–1960), *Cora Sandel* (1880–1974), *Aksel Sandemose* (1899–1965), *Tarjei Vesaas* (1897–1970) and *Johan Borgen* (1902–).

Bjørnson, Hamsun and Undset have been awarded the Nobel Prize in literature.

The Oseberg Viking ship from approx. 850 A. D. at Vikingskiphuset in Oslo.

Book Publishing

Although Norway is one of the world's smallest language communities, it is also one of the countries which annually has the greatest number of books published per capita. Non-periodicals (more than 49 pages, reprints included) annually number about 2,500 titles, about 2/3 of which are of Norwegian origin. The total number of books and pamphlets printed in one year is nearly 20 mill.

Norwegian authors deal directly with their publishers without employing agents as middlemen. Standard contracts are customary, securing the author a certain royalty percentage of the sales of the book.

Libraries

The library system in Norway is organized with government-subsidized public libraries all over the country. A good library is found in most cities and other densely populated areas. In 1973 the number of volumes in 4,835 public and school libraries totalled 13,4 mill. with an annual issue of 17,7 mill. books.

The university and college libraries have a total of 5.0 mill. volumes, other scientific and public institutions, various associations, commercial libraries etc. 2.9 mill. volumes. The University Library in Oslo with faculty libraries is the largest with about 3,0 mill. volumes, in addition to 46.173 bindings of newspapers, 90.000 map sheets, 18,900 scripts, notations, and 111,500 scores.

Theatre

It was not until 1827 in Oslo and 1850 in Bergen that the country's first permanent stages were opened, and during the period 1860–70 Norwegian theatres became fully national and independent. The building of the *National Theatre* in Oslo was of the greatest significance, and since its opening in 1899 this has been Norway's main stage. The *National Stage* in Bergen has also had great influence on the development and history of Norwegian theatre. Many of the country's greatest actors have started their career on this stage.

The form and style of Norwegian theatre have been profoundly influenced by the dramas of *Henrik Ibsen* and *Bjørnstjerne Bjørnson*. Both these two great authors were stimulating theatre managers and producers. Other Norwegian and foreign authors have naturaly also given important impulses to the Norwegian theatre.

There are today permanent stages in Oslo, Bergen, Trondheim *(Trøndelag Theatre)*, Stavanger *(Rogaland Theatre)*, Tromsø *(Hålogaland Theatre)*, Skien *(Telemark theatre)* and Molde *(The Regional Theatre of Møre and Romsdal)*.

Other cities and rural districts are dependent on touring shows by the permanent theatres. Since 1949 the *Norwegian State Travelling Theatre* (Riksteatret) has organized tours all over the country. As the name implies, this theatre is a State undertaking, with a board and a director appointed by the King in Council. About 800 performances are given annually by Riksteateret. Government subsidies: 11,6 mill. kroner.

Seven of Norway's theatres (two in Oslo) are subsidized equally by the government and the respective municipalities. Government subsidies to theatres amounted to 37.2 mill. kroner in 1974.

Music

Finds of instruments from the Bronze Age prove that the exceptionally rich and varied Norwegian folk music has old traditions, although this music to a great extent originates from medieval church music. Folk music is still an important factor in cultural life, especially in the rural districts, and has always been a source of inspiration to Norwegian composers. The national instruments are, first, the "Hardanger fiddle», then a string instrument called "Langeleik", and "Lur", a long wind instrument made of birch bark. Every Sunday afternoon the Norwegian Broadcasting Corporation has programs of Norwegian folk music.

Ole Bull (1810–80), the violin virtuoso, was the first Norwegian musician to attain international fame. He enraptured the Old and the New World with improvisations on Norwegian folk music. *Edvard Grieg* (1843–1907) and *Johan Svendsen* (1840–1911) in the 1860s composed music which for many decades greatly influenced the development of Norwegian music. Grieg is indisputably Norway's greatest composer. Although his music has definite national characteristics, it is also universal, and his compositions have won recognition and are played all over the world.

Other outstanding composers include *Johan Halvorsen, Halfdan Kjerulf, Christian Sinding, Rikard Nordraak* and *Agathe Backer Grøndahl*. Of modern composers, *Ludvig Irgens Jensen, Klaus Egge, Eivind Groven, Fartein Valen*, who has

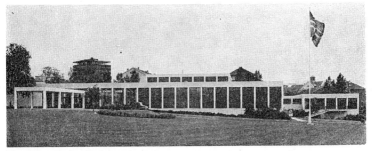

The Edvard Munch Museum in Oslo.

created a personal atonal style, *Arne Eggen*, *Bjarne Brustad*, *Geirr Tveitt*, *David Monrad Johansen*, *Olav Kielland* and *Harald Sæverud*, are the most prominent. *Arne Norheim*, *Egil Hovland* and *Finn Mortensen* are the most important contemporary composers. *Øivin Fjeldstad* and *Karsten Andersen* are often guest conductors abroad.

Among active musicians the names of *Robert Riefling*, *Kjell Bækkelund* and *Liv Glaser* (pianists), *Aase Nordmo Løvberg* and *Ingrid Bjoner* (sopranos) and the violinist *Arve Tellefsen* are probably best known abroad. *Kaja Eide Norena* and *Kirsten Flagstad* were both sopranos of world-wide fame.

Norwegians are very interested in music. Orchestras, choirs and bands are formed even in rural districts and small towns. A number of guest musicians and singers contribute to interesting concert seasons.

International summer festivals are held annually in Bergen, and jazz festivals in Molde and Kongsberg.

Four orchestras (in Oslo, Bergen, Trondheim and Stavanger) receive government and municipal subsidies as well as regular fees from the Norwegian Broadcasting Corporation.

Opera

The Norwegian Opera (Den norske opera) is a very young institution, founded 1958 with the famous singer *Kirsten Flagstad* as its first manager.

The Norwegian opera is a national company. Its permanent stage is in Oslo, but performances are also given at other places in the country where the necessary facilities for stage and orchestra can be provided, economic aspects also being taken into consideration.

Shareholders in the opera company are the Government (50 shares), the city of Oslo (40 shares) and the Norwegian Opera Fund (10 shares). The Government and the municipality of Oslo each provide 50 % of the necessary subsidies, which in 1974 totalled about 24,6 mill. kroner.

Film

Only about 6 – 8 films are produced in Norway p.a., and most of them are intended for the home market. Only a couple of the films produced here since the end of the second world war have aroused interest outside Norway.

With such a limited market, Norwegian film producers have to rely on Government subsidies. In 1973, the subsidy for film production amounted to about 10.5 million kroner. A Norwegian black-and-white film gets a subsidy equivalent to 45 per cent of gross box office receipts; in the case of colour films and other rather expensive productions, 55 per cent of production costs are covered. Furthermore, producers may apply for state guarantee on productions covering 80 – 90 per cent of total production costs. Average expenditure on a Norwegian film (1973) amounts to about N.kr 1.3 million. Special guarantees are given to short films, mainly documentary and educational films, but also to experimental films and to children's films. About 70–80 short films are produced annually.

All films which are to be shown to the general public have to be submitted to Statens Filmsensur (The Government Board of Censors), as laid down by Kinoloven (The Cinema Act) of 1913. Censorship is concentrated principally on brutality, sadism, terror and pornography.

Under the Cinema Act also local authorities may run cinemas, and under that Act a network of municipal cinemas has been authorised. Today there are about 200 municipal cinemas in Norway, with a total seating capacity of 84,000. The number of private cinemas is somewhat in excess of this, but most of them are small, and are situated in rural districts. Municipal cinemas represent approximately 80 per cent of annual gross box office receipts.

Vigelandsanlegget, The Vigeland sculpture park in Oslo, is well known for all tourists visiting Oslo.

Fine Arts

In a European context Norwegian art was at its peak during the period 700–1300 A.D.

The unique, completely preserved Viking ship (approx. 850 A.D.), the richly carved wagons, sleighs and other objects of art found in the burial mound at *Oseberg*, are the most important extant evidence of the highranking pictorial and ornamental art of the Viking period. Through finds of jewelry, this art may be traced to Christian times (from approx. 1000 A.D.) when it soon merged with European ornamentation in Romanesque design. *The stave church portals* (1000–1200 A.D.) are outstanding examples of the quality of this ornamental art and the further evolution of old Norse tradition. At the same time the Church introduced a new non-ornamental pictorial art. A number of sculptures from before 1200 A.D. have been preserved. The oldest preserved paintings date from the 13th century: a number of painted altar pieces in Gothic style show mainly English influence. As *the first known examples of oil painting* they also claim international interest. From the same period there are wall decorations and ceiling paintings in the stave churches.

Early and late Gothic sculpture flourished in Scandinavia, and the sculptural ornamentation of the Cathedral of Trondheim was of great artistic importance. A considerable number of wooden sculptures from this period have been preserved in Norway, and the crucifixes, Madonna images and statues of St. Olav are all of a high quality.

Beautiful picture tapestries were woven in the Middle Ages. The

Baldishol tapestry (about 1180) is a magnificent specimen, and has the months of April and May as its theme.

The period of national decline coincided with a stagnation in art, and from the late Middle Ages only imported works of significance have been preserved. The art of the Renaissance and Baroque periods, compared with that of the Middle Ages, is of a more provincial nature. However, particularly during the period 1700 till the 1850s, many enchanting works of folk art were produced, in wood carving, decorative oil painting *(rosemaling)* and pictural weaving alike.

Modern Painting

A revival of Norwegian art did not take place until about 1800 with the painter *Johan Chr. Dahl*. Having lived mostly in Germany, he was strongly influenced by German Romanticism, but his conception of Norwegian motifs was deeply personal. Dahl was the first great painter of Norwegian landscapes, and it was he who again brought Norwegian art in close contact with the currents of Europe. *Thomas Fearnley* (1802–40) was the most prominent of his pupils.

The next generation took different paths, into the period of National Romanticism, with idealized landscapes and depictions. The greatest talent of that period, *Lars Hertevig* (1830–1902), lived and died unregarded. During a few years, before his creative power was paralysed by insanity, he painted unique «timeless» and expressive landscapes.

In the 1880s, the period of Naturalism, a new talented generation appeared, with *Christian Krohg* (1852 –1925) and *Erik Werenskiold* (1855- 1938) as the dominating personalities, and *Frits Thaulow* (1847–1906) as the most popular – also abroad. All three were to influence the young *Edvard Munch*.

Harriet Backer (1845–1932), who held a more modest place, is today considered one of the greatest talents in painting Norway ever had. *Halfdan Egedius* (1877–99), a child prodigy of the Neo-Romantic period, and the remarkable painter *Harald Sohlberg* (1869–1935) were of the same generation. Around the turn of century the «colour poets» *Oluf Wold Torne* (1867–1919) and *Thorvald Erichsen* (1868–1939) won fame.

The most famous of all is *Edvard Munch* (1863–1944), one of the few Norwegians who have influenced the evolution of European art. His highly personal style laid the foundation of modern Expressionism. His paintings of «studies of modern spiritual life» demonstrate what he described as the Frieze of Life («The Shriek», «Dance of Life», «Vampire» and others). The principal work from his later period is the decoration of the Aula of the University of Oslo (1910–16). Edvard Munch is one of the greatest masters of graphic art. His works may be studied at the National Gallery and at the Munch Museum in Oslo, and at the Rasmus Meyer Gallery in Bergen.

Contemporary Art

A dominating feature of our own century is mural painting. With the exception of Mexico, there is hardly any other country in the world where in recent days frescoes have flourished as they have in Norway. The artists include *Axel Revold* (1887–1962, main work: Bergens Privatbank, Bergen); *Per Krogh* (1889 –1965, main work: Seamen's School, Oslo, and UN-building, New York); *Alf Rolfsen* (b. 1895, main work: Western Crematorium, Oslo). A central personality is *Henrik Sørensen* (1882–1962), expressing the mystical in nature as well as social and religious pathos. All four have painted murals in Oslo City Hall. *Rolf Nesch* (1893– 1975) is probably the most famous of our contemporary artists with his modern and eversurprising assemblages. A kindred expression is found in the works of *Sigurd Winge* (1909- 1970)and *Paul René Gauguin* (1910–

1976). *Kai Fjell* (b. 1907) has made an original contribution to the romantic tradition in Norwegian painting, a tradition which is also felt in some works of non-figurative art, such as those of *Knut Rumohr* (b. 1916) and *Jakob Weidemann* (b. 1923). Today Norwegian graphic art has a wide scope. During the last decades pictorial weaving has flourished; remarkable artists are *Hannah Ryggen* (1894–1970) and *Synnøve Aurdal* (b. 1908).

Sculpture

From an international point of view, recent Norwegian sculpture is hardly of the same interest as the other fields of pictorial art.

The best known, and undoubtedly the most talented sculptor, is *Gustav Vigeland* (1869–1943). His genius is primarily expressed in monuments and portrait busts from the first two decades of our own century. Although his working power was that of a genius all his life, he lacked moderation and self-criticism. The gigantic array of sculptures in the Frogner Park, Oslo (the Vigeland Museum) gives the impression of a virtually incomprehensible over-production.

In many respects Vigeland overshadowed his contemporaries. One of those was *Ingebrigt Vik* (1867–1928; museum at Øystese, Hardanger).

The generation between the two World Wars is widely represented in the decoration of the Oslo City Hall. One of the most prominent decorators is *Anne Grimdalen*, who inter alia is the creator of the stylized equestrian statue on the western wall.

After World War II many war memorials have been erected. One of the most interesting from an artistic point of view is the one in Bergen by *Hans Jacob Meyer* (b. 1907).

Among our contemporary sculptors there is a wide scope of expression, ranging from the Naturalism of *Per Palle Storm* (b. 1910) to the non-figuration of *Arnold Haukeland* (b. 1920). The latter has inter alia

created several daring abstracts in stainless steel. A competition in early 1967 for a statue of King Haakon VII was won by *Nils Aas* (b. 1933).

Architecture

Norway's most characteristic contribution to Medieval architecture is the wooden stave churches. The original number was about 800, of which 30 have been more or less completely preserved. In addition to the building of stave churches there was a rich stone architecture. The *Cathedral of Trondheim* is the most important example of the latter. It is the most northern Gothic cathedral in the world, and a national shrine. The oldest parts of it (Anglo-Norman style) date from about 1150 A. D. The Cathedral was completed around 1320 A. D. in the Gothic style, but a number of fires left it partly in ruins. A complete restoration was commenced in 1869.

Other churches to be mentioned are the *Old Aker Church* in Oslo about 1100 A.D., the *Maria Church* in Bergen, and the *Stavanger Cathedral* (Romanesque nave approx. 1130–50, High Gothic choir approx. 1280).

Håkonshallen in Bergen (completed 1261) is the most outstanding example of secular buildings from this period.

The fine craftmanship of the Middle Ages is expressed in buildings of timber, dating from the 13th century and later.

The mighty *Rosenkrantz Tower* in Bergen (approx. 1560) and the two manor houses *Austråt* and *Rosendal* (around 1650–60) are the most important buildings from the Renaissance and Baroque periods. In the 18th century wood architecture had a very flourishing period, with the large *Stiftsgården* in Trondheim as the most splendid example.

After 1814

Norway's rebirth as an independent nation resulted in great building

The Nidaros Cathedral in Trondheim is Norway's national shrine.

activities. Leading architects at that time were *H. D. F. Linstow* (1787–1851, The Royal Palace in Oslo) and *Chr. H. Grosch* (1801–1865, Oslo University and other public buildings).

Among the main buildings of the Romantic period are *Nebelong's* castle Oscarshall (1850) and *Langlet's* Parliament building (1860s) in Oslo.

The first part of the 20th century architecture was still greatly influenced by National-Romantic trends, the two leading architects being *Arnstein Arneberg* (1882–1961) and *Magnus Poulsson* (1881–1958), whose joint main work is the Oslo City Hall (1916–50).

The influence of modern architectural trends did not reach Norway until about 1930, represented by architects such as *Ove Bang* (1895–1942) and *Arne Korsmo* (1900–1968). The period after 1945 is particularly dominated by housing architecture, although several important buildings in a more monumental style have been built. Striking examples are *Erling Viksjø's* (1910–1971) Government Building, Bakkehaugen Church,

and the Head Office of Norsk Hydro, all in Oslo.

Among the most interesting buildings from recent years we may include the Franciscan Monastery and the St. Hallvard Church in Oslo (both erected in 1966), of which the architects were *Kjell Lund* (1927–) and *Nils Slaatto* (1923–). The monumental Municipal Hall of Asker is another example of their joint work.

Applied Arts and Design

Rich grave finds from the Viking Age around 1000 A.D. show that even at that time Norwegians had a great sense of beauty, colour and form and liked to surround themselves with beautiful things. Today this sense of quality has become even more established.

Arts and crafts and industrial design flourish side by side in Norway, complementing and influencing each other. The simple, exquisite and functional forms from Norway are based on traditions and experience through centuries.

Arts and Crafts

The many prizes awarded Norway at applied art exhibitions prove that the Norwegian applied art is well prepared to meet the increasing competition.

Enamelware is a Norwegian speciality. It seems that the artistic disposition of the Norwegians has found a characteristic medium of expression in the bright, vivid colours of the enamel. Together with silver or gold, copper or stainless steel, enamel creates beautiful effects, in jewelry as well as ware such as tea spoons and salad sets, just to mention a few examples. In this respect tribute should be paid to *Grete Prytz Korsmo*, of whom it may be said that the great renaissance in Norwegian enamel art is due. Through extensive research she has paved the way for Norwegian enamel to its present leading position.

Lately jewelry combining silver

with Norwegian stones like ama-
zonite and rock crystals has met
with great success.

Textiles have a rich background in
national traditions. Old techniques
are used to express a new sense of
design in tapestries, carpets and rugs.

Furniture has become an important
export article, reaching a figure of
220 mill. kroner in 1973. This success
is due to a high level of crafts-
manship in models of contemporary
elegance. Here, as in the case of other
applied arts in Norway, there has
been a certain continuity of crafts-
manship, good design and ambition
to transform the individual home into
something more than a dwelling place.

Industrial Design

The general design standard is very
high. Industries in the applied art
sector cooperate extensively with
designers of furniture, glassware,
earthenware, ceramics, textiles and
precious and non-precious metals.

There are about 50 industrial
designers in Norway who are members of the organization Norwegian
Industrial Designers (ID). This professional group in turn belongs to
the Norwegian Society of Arts and
Crafts and Industrial Design (Lands-
forbundet Norsk Brukskunst) which
aims, inter alia, «to improve the
quality, in practical and artistic
terms, of industrial, handicraft and
homecraft products and to bring
about greater understanding for
and the increased use of good
design in the home, at work and in
society at large».

Government Support

The government finances or provides economic support for art gal-
leries and exhibitions of plastic art,
operas, orchestras, music festivals
and academies, theatres, film production, public libraries, museums
and archives.

The Norwegian Cultural Fund was
established by a Parliamentary act
of 1964 and has a consultative council of 11 members, appointed for a
4 years period. Grants to art and
culture preservation are approved
by the King on the advice of the
Council, which will also have at its
disposal sums for immediate support
of projects or for its own initiatives.
These decisions are to be sanctioned
by the Ministry of Church and Education.

The statutes originally provided
that the yearly grants to the Fund
should be at least a sum correspon-
ding to the revenue of the purchase
tax on periodicals and weeklies (introduced 1965, estimated at 15 mill.
kroner). In 1967 purchase tax on
weeklies and books was abolished.
(By 1970 the new value-added tax was
put on weeklies, not on books). But
from 1967 the appropriations to the
Fund are voted upon by Parliament
independently of any revenue.

Government appropriations to the
Fund in 1975 amounted to 30 mill.
kroner. Approx. 7.3 mill. was allocated to literature, 2.4 mill. to
music, 4 mill. to pictorial art, 3.4
mill. to culture preservation, 9,2
mill. to buildings and 3,7 mill. to
periodicals, reports, promotion of
Lappish culture, film etc.

Other Allocations

Government grants to authors and
artists are awarded in various forms:

1) *Life grants* 15,000 kroner (in
1973: 25 fellowships).

2) *Honorary annuity* (in 1975:
kr 40,000).

3) *Grants for a 3 years' period:*
24,000 kroner (in 1975: 100).

4) *Grants for a 3 years' period:*
7,000 kroner (in 1975: 21).

5) *Scholarships for studies abroad*
(in 1975: 5 of 20,000 kroner and
35 of 10,000 kroner).

6) *Scholarships for stage managers:*
(in 1975: 2 of 12,500 kroner.)

7) *Scholarships for pictorial artists:*
(in 1975: 7 of 2,000 kroner).

8) *Life grants for senior artists:*
8,000 (in 1975: 73). Total 1975:
4,976,000 kroner.

Religion

The Evangelical Lutheran Church is the State (Established) Church of Norway (Art. 2 of the Constitution). There is, however, complete freedom of religion, enabling all members of dissenting churches to worship in accordance with their faith. The Established Church is endowed by the State. In accordance with a law passed in 1969, the State also supports the officially registered free churches.

The country is divided into 10 Dioceses. These are subdivided into 91 Deaneries, 591 Clerical districts and 1,067 Parishes. Services are held in more than 1,450 churches and chapels, served by approximately 1,100 clergymen. The clergy are appointed by the King-in-Council.

A Law passed in 1938 gave women formal and legal right to become ministers of the Church of Norway. In 1961 the Cabinet appointed the first woman minister of the Church.

About 96 % of the population belong to the Church of Norway. Membership of various free churches, such as Pentecost congregations, Free Church Lutherans, Methodists, Baptists, Roman Catholics and others, totals about 150,000.

All offices performed by the Church such as baptism, confirmation, wedding and funeral ceremonies are free of charge to members of the Church. The salaries and pensions of church servants are paid by the government. More than 80 % of all marriages are performed by the Church. Baptism and confirmation are almost universal, and funerals (burials and cremations) are practically always solemnized by ministers of the Church.

Numerous religious organizations support and supplement the work of the Established Church, through lay services by travelling evangelists, Sunday schools, Bible schools etc., as well as financial aid, publishing of religious books etc.

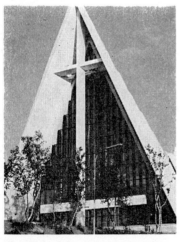

The Tromsdalen Church in Tromsø, Northern Norway, was consecrated in 1966. It is also known as «the Cathedral of the Arctic Ocean».

Missionary Work

Norwegian missionaries have been very active abroad, especially in Asia and Africa. Norway is the country which, in proportion to population, has the highest number of missionaries. There are altogether 27 missionary organizations, with more than 2,000 missionaries in the field, serving congregations of about half a million baptized members. Total contributions to Christian missionary work in foreign countries amount to 130 mill. kroner per year.

Sports and Recreation

Outdoor Recreation

Outdoor life and sports play a very important part in the life of every Norwegian. Even residents of the larger cities may easily and cheaply reach a countryside suited for recreation.

Few capitals can offer their inhabitants facilities for out-of-door recreation like Oslo, which is surrounded by forests and peaceful lakes, covering about a quarter of a million acres. This area, called *Oslomarka*, has a network of innumerable ski trails during the winter and walking paths in summer.

Norway is a country where you still may wander through country unspoiled by man. Summer holidays are spent in the mountains or at the coast, while the mass «evacuation» from the cities to the mountains for Easter skiing is a unique Norwegian habit.

The favourite form for *skiing* in Norway is to take cross-country trips through the hilly woodlands, while downhill and slalom have a more limited following.

The shortness of the Nordic winter day is a hindrance to participation in skiing after working hours. However, this is gradually being remedied through the illumination of ski trails. About 700 ski trails in various parts of the country are now flood-lit by electric lamps.

In the summer time sea water temperature generally permits *swimming* along the coast from June until the end of August. All types of boats, ranging from yachts to kayaks, provide recreation and fun for all who spend their holidays at the sea.

Fresh water fishing and *mountaineering* are sports for which the Norwegian countryside is particularly well suited and which for many years have attracted visitors from abroad. Trout and salmon rivers are found practically all along the coast, and on the mountain plateau of the interior trout fishing is often excellent.

Possibilities for *game shooting* are also good. It is estimated that about 1,300,000 animals, big game and small game are shot annually in Norway. The figures for 1974 are: 8,600 elks, 4,000 wild reindeer, and 3,400 red deer. Between 100,000 and 700,000 grouse (ptarmigan) are shot annually, and about 65,000 hares. Information on hunting and fishing in Norway may be obtained from *Norges Jeger- og Fiskerforbund* (Norwegian Hunters' and Anglers' Association), Grønlandsleiret 39, Oslo.

Mountain peaks have challenged the skill and daring of *climbers* from all over the world. Some of the more spectacular first ascents have been made by French mountaineers. Both mountaineers as well as hikers preferring less exacting surroundings will find a number of tourist cabins offering hospitality and accommodation ranging from hotel comfort to simple bunks.

Competitive Sports

Norwegians are generally greatly interested in sports and competitions. *Norges Idrettsforbund* (Norwegian Confederation of Sports) has 7,214 clubs and a direct membership of 957,484, (1975). The Confederation's 39 associations comprehend a wide variety of sports. *The Football Association* (319,175 members) and the *Ski Association* (214,100 members) are the largest of these branch associations.

Sports are given financial support by the government, the means being provided by a government football pool company (Norsk Tipping) which has a monopoly on football betting in Norway. About one third of total profits of the pool are allocated to promotion of sports. There are 5,000 sports grounds

There is no age limit for skiers. The participants in this race already have the true competitive spirit.

and about 2,000 ski jumping hills. The number of indoor swimming pools is steadily increasing, but there are very few artifical skating rinks. In this connection, however, it should be remembered that most lakes are covered with ice all winter and thereby offer good facilities for skating.

Summer Sports

Football is easily the most popular game in Norway, being played all over the country. Championships and international matches attract capacity crowds.

Athletic sports competitions also have considerable following, and Olympic and European championships have often been won by Nor-

wegians. *Sailing* is very popular along the coast, and Norwegian yachtsmen, among them the King and the Crown Prince, have won international recognition.

Other summer sports include *shooting, swimming, rowing, canoeing, cycling, handball, tennis, badminton, golf, archery,* and *orientation.*

Many American and European games such as baseball, cricket, rugby, squash and lacrosse are not played in Norway. Indoor sports such as *wrestling, boxing* and *gymnastics* are popular.

Winter Sports

Skiing is the national sport of Norway, and Norwegians call their country the «cradle of skiing». Although this may be some slight exaggeration, the Nordic forms for skiing, such as jumping and cross country, are considered to have originated in this country. Norway's strength in winter sports is illustated by the results of the Olympic Winter Games, in which Norwegians during the years 1924–76 have won 141 medals, far more than any other nation.

Cross country races and *jumping* contests are held regularly from December until April. *Slalom* and *downhill* are gaining an increasing following from young people. The climax of the skiing season is the *Holmenkoll competition* in mid-March, where top skiers from the whole world compete with the native champions in jumping, cross country, slalom and downhill.

Speed skating is also a national sport. In figure skating Sonja Henie (1912–1969) is the outstanding representative, with 3 Olympic and 10 consecutive world championships during the years 1927–36.

Tourism in Norway

Most tourists visit Norway to see its magnificient scenery and enjoy the great outdoors. In spite of Norway's geographical location the climate is favourable in summer as well as in winter. The greatest attractions during the summer months are the midnight sun, the fjords, mountains and waterfalls. Mountain plateaus and rivers provide unlimited possibilities for hiking and fishing during the summer months. Norwegian mountain resorts are the destination of many winter sports enthusiasts. Popular seaside areas have also been developed along the fjords and in recent years these have become important tourist centres.

Tourism began in earnest in Norway around 1860. It is uncertain how many tourists actually visit Norway each year since complete statistics are not available, but the figure is up the millions when travellers from Nordic neighbouring countries are included. Revenues from tourism amounted to 1,600 million kroner in 1973.

About 550 transport companies along with the Norwegian State Railways and the airlines SAS (Scandinavian Airlines System) and Braathens SAFE handle the tourist traffic. There are about 450 hotels/motels and 1,700 other inns and boarding houses available for tourists, but many visitors prefer the camping sites and simple camping cottages or tents when travelling by car with a family.

From an economic point of view tourism is an auxiliary industry. Only in some of the more distinct tourist districts does it become more of a main source of livelihood. The travel companies and hotels benefit from the extra business and tourism represents a supplemental source of income for many farmers and business people in more sparsely populated areas. It also contributes to maintaining the pattern of scattered settlements which is so characteristic for Norway.

Standard of Living

Incomes

Since World War II and up till 1973 the rise in total private income per capita has been nearly eightfolded and in real terms nearly tripled. The share in real income, which has been transferred by government to households in the form of sickness benefits, old age pensions, childrens benefits and other social amenities has been doubled during the period 1946–1973. During the same period private disposable income (total private income, less direct taxes) has been nearly ninefolded, while the disposable real income has been nearly tripled.

After World War II there has been a great change in the distribution of income, this being to a great extent due to the great demand for skilled labour, resulting in higher wages. However, it is a fact that the highly progressive taxation of high and medium level incomes, together with the social benefits which are mainly allocated according to needs, have been greatly instrumental in equalizing incomes. While the majority of incomes prior to World War II were in the low bracket, in 1973 most incomes were relatively close to median.

Private Consumption

Private consumption constituted in 1973 an average of 88 per cent of disposable income, compared with 90 per cent shortly after World War II.

The changes in quantities of the various types of consumer goods as shown in the table below, confirm that Norway is well on its way towards becoming an affluent society.

Consumption per head in percentage of total consumption:

	1946	1973
Food	30.5	22,8
Beverages and tobacco.	11.2	7,7
Rent, light and fuel ...	11.7	13,8
Clothing and footwear	13.1	9,3
Household goods	5.9	7,8
Medical expend. and personal care.......	5.9	8,5
Travel and transportation	4.7	12,1
Leisure and education	4.7	7,1
Other goods and services...........	12.3	10,9
Total...............	100.0	100.0

The declining share of the food, beverages and tobacco sector shows that in Norway the saturation point is reached, and that demand is instead

being directed towards commodities such as furniture, household goods, and goods and services which make life more pleasant. The variety of foods on the market has greatly increased with emphasis on fancy foods. Self-service stores, following the American pattern, are taking the place of the small grocers and drapers. Nearly 100 per cent of all homes have electricity, which is also very cheap. A wide range of electric household appliances are in general use, with deep freeze cabinets, home coffee grinders and heated swimming-pools as the latest status symbols. The increased share of the travel and transportation sector, mainly private cars, is also an indication of affluence. Purchase of automobiles and related expenses rose from one per cent in 1946 to seven per cent in 1968. The greatest increase in the number of automobiles took place after 1959. Up to 1975 the number of inhabitants per automobile fell from 21 to 4,2.

One of the government's primary targets has been to stimulate the building of good dwellings. About three fourth of the dwellings completed are financed by loans from the State Housing Bank and the State Agricultural Bank. Such loans have very easy repayment terms, and the rate of interest is moderate. There is also a current housing subsidy for families with children, elderly and handicapped people. The subsidy is calculated on the basis of actual income and housing expenditure of the household for families with incomes below certain levels. From 1946 to 1974 about 850,000 dwellings were built, which means that 60 per cent of all the households live in houses built in this period. However, due to rising income and internal migration, there is still a housing shortage especially in the bigger towns.

It is stipulated by law that ordinary working hours shall not exceed 9 hours a day and 42.5 hours a week. In certain jobs working hours are shorter (regular shift work, mine workers and workers in tunnel work, working underground). For agricultural workers (agriculture, forestry associated with agriculture, livestock, farming, furfarming, horticulture and gardening), act of 19th December 1958 provides that ordinary working hours shall not exceed 8 hours a day and 48 hours a week. The Act also places rigid requirements on employers to implement measures protecting against accidents and injuries, and also includes legislation protecting women workers duduring pregnancy and after confinement. Special regulations are given to protect young workers and children.

Wage earners are by law also entitled to 4 weeks holiday with somewhat more than full wages. To be free on Saturdays in return for longer working hours during the week is, in agreement with the employer and labour organizations, common practice in industry, business and civil service.

The century-established practice of unrestricted right of wayfare across water and uncultivated land is also established by law. This provides holidaymakers and tourists with cars and caravans, or on foot or bicycle abundant possibilities for recreation.

Family and consumer affairs

A separate Ministry of Family and Consumer Affairs was established as early as 1956. In 1972 the Ministry's functions were transferred to the new *Ministry of Consumer Affairs and Government Administration, the Family and Consumer Department.* Increasingly greater attention has been focused on the question of consumer policy in our society, and there is broad political consensus concerning a greater effort in the fields of research, consumer information, protection and influence.

The agencies under the jurisdiction of the Family and Consumer Department include the *Consumer Council,* the *Committee for Declaration of Contents and Quality Marking,* the *State Institute of Consumer Research*

The mountains of Norway are a paradise for vacationers.

and Testing of Goods as well as the *Consumer Ombudsman* and the *Market Council.* These are represented in national as well as international bodies.

Information to consumers is provided through the school system, special courses, the consumers' direct contact with the various consumer institutions and perhaps, most important, through the mass media and the information accompanying each piece of merchandise. Efforts are being made to arrive at methods for increasing the consumer's direct influence on product development and the production of goods and supply of services.

The council with which the consumers are most familiar is the *Consumer Council* whose most important task is to safeguard the interests of consumers. The council publishes a magazine *Consumer Reports* which appears ten times a year with a circulation of 260,000. The magazine publishes results of comparative product surveys and presents other

77

material of general interest to consumers, including information on legal aspects of consumer sales, various services, advertising, the environment, pollution, etc.

The main task of the *Committee for Declaration of Contents and Quality Marking* is to work for the implementation of a practical system for the labelling of merchandise for those product categories where consumers have a need for information.

The objective of the *State Institute of Consumer Research and Testing of Goods* is to study various consumer questions from the users' point of view. This is carried out on the basis of research and product surveys.

The *Consumer Ombudsman* and the *Market Council* are the most recent additions to the consumer field. Activities began in 1973 and the purpose of these institutions is to safeguard the interests of both consumers and business people and to stimulate sound marketing conditions.

All of the consumer institutions carry out an extensive information programme.

Environmental protection

In Norway the coordination of environmental measures, including the responsibility for physical planning, pollution matters, nature conservation and recreational areas as well as international cooperation in these fields, is handled by the Ministry of Environment. The Ministry was established in May 1972. As in a number of other countries, Norway's general principle in the field of environmental protection is that those responsible for pollution shall pay.

Even though Norway is located in the periphery of industrialized Europe, the country is also influenced by sources of pollution from outside the country's borders. The increasing emission of sulpher dioxide today represents a serious environmental problem in Norway. It is generally recognized that air pollution under special weather conditions can be transferred over sizeable distances. The increased acidity of precipitation in Norway is therefore closely related to the increasingly greater pollution in Central Europe and Great Britain. Norway is also involved in efforts to safeguard the resources of the sea against pollution and participates actively in the development of international environmental measures.

Activities on the Norwegian continental shelf in connection with oil drilling and production also necessitate the establishment of a comprehensive system of control and supervision of pollution in these ocean areas.

Books on Norway in Eglish

Askeland, Jan: Norwegian painting. A survey. Oslo 1971, Tanum.

Helvig, Magne og Viggo Johannessen: Norway. Land – people – industries. A brief geography. Oslo 1970, Tanum.

Hove, Olav: The system of education in Norway. Oslo 1968, Tanum.

Jerman, Gunnar: New Norway. '74. Publ. by the Export council of Norway. Oslo 1973, Grøndahl.

Knudsen, Ole: Norway at work. A survey of the principal branches of the economy. Oslo 1972, Tanum.

Lange, Kristian: Norwegian music. A survey. Oslo 1971, Tanum.

Midgaard, John: A brief history of Norway. Oslo 1971, Tanum.

Motoring in Norway. Publ. by Norway travel association. Oslo 1972, Bokcentralen.

Nesheim, Asbjørn: Introducing the lapps. Oslo 1963, Tanum.

Parmann, Øistein: Norwegian sculpture. Oslo 1969, Dreyer.

Tourist in Norway. Text: Erling Welle-Strand. Oslo 1974, Schibsted.

Tourist in Oslo. Ed. Svein Ellingsen. Oslo 1971, Schibsted.

678 14 676 2250